The
BRIDGE to
BRILLIANCE

The
BRIDGE to
BRILLIANCE

HOW ONE PRINCIPAL
IN A TOUGH COMMUNITY
IS INSPIRING THE WORLD

NADIA LOPEZ

with Rebecca Paley

VIKING

VIKING
An imprint of Penguin Random House LLC
375 Hudson Street
New York, New York 10014
penguin.com

Hardcover ISBN 9781101980255
E-book ISBN 9781101980279

Printed in the United States of America
10 9 8 7 6 5 4 3 2 1

Set in ITC Esprit

This book is dedicated to:

My daughter, Cenné, and my parents for the gift of life

The community of Brownsville and District 23 for sharing your *"Brilliance"*

Educators everywhere—stay encouraged

My job as principal is not only to educate children but also to protect them. While I have been completely truthful in this book about my experience starting a school in Brownsville, certain names and identifying biographical details have been changed (in one case, a composite character was created) in order to protect the identities of not only students but also family members and teachers.

CONTENTS

PREFACE

Sitting at my desk, I contemplated all the paperwork that had piled up since my school, Mott Hall Bridges Academy, was thrust into the spotlight a few months before. A small public middle school in one of the poorest and most underserved neighborhoods of Brooklyn was an unlikely candidate for an international press sensation. But ever since one of my boys brought attention to Mott Hall through a comment he made on the popular blog *Humans of New York,* ordinary people around the world had been captivated by what I was trying to do—which was simply to take care of kids everyone else seemed to want to forget.

I had barely started on the stack of performance reviews awaiting my attention when Malik walked in and sat down in one of the chairs across from my desk. The kids in this building know my door is open to them any-time.

"I need to have a talk," the sixth grader said in such a soft voice I could hardly hear him.

"Talk about what?" I asked.

"About me."

"What about you?"

"My work."

"What about it?"

"It's hard."

"Okay, which classes are hard for you?"

"Every class. Except PE. It's too hard. I'm failing. I always fail."

His problems had begun back in his elementary school when his fourth-grade teachers, who couldn't tolerate his angry demeanor, let him fall behind.

Malik, with chubby cheeks from baby fat he'd soon lose and sad eyes that he kept downcast, was typical of a kid from a failing elementary school; he was two years older than most of the children in his grade because he'd been held back a couple of times. The first thing people notice about him is that he looks like he's angry—all the time. His expression makes it seem like he can't be bothered, like he doesn't want to hear what you have to say. That couldn't be further from the truth, but you would never know it unless you speak to him, which his expression keeps people from doing. I always tell my kids, "You need to understand there are teachers in this world who, if they don't like you, have that power to derail you. Even if you don't feel like they're invested, you can't stop doing your work. Because they will be fine with you failing and repeating the grade."

I understood how Malik's demeanor could deflate a whole room and how frustrating that might be for a teacher just trying to get through a curriculum that was necessary to prepare a class to take state exams. But it wasn't that he didn't care; he *acted* like he didn't care. Some teachers in his elementary school, however, took his negative behavior personally. Instead of supporting him and working with him until he understood the material, they just held him over. That started a trajectory from which it would be very hard for Malik to deviate.

Making kids repeat grades unfortunately is rarely about remediation and more about punishment. So when Malik came to us, not only did he still lack the academic skills he should have had by sixth grade but, as a thirteen-year-old in class with mostly eleven-year-olds, he was also disconnected from his peers. He would become agitated by how loud the other children in his class, who were at a different maturity and energy level, would get.

Don't mistake me, Malik was not innocent. Soon after he arrived at Mott Hall, he had to call his mother from my office because he was talking back to his teacher and arguing with his peers. He got on the phone and said, "Yeah.

So I'm told I need to call you because, like, I was rude. Yeah. Uh-huh. Uh-huh. Yeah, a'ight." Then he hung up.

"Who were you talking to?" I asked.

"My mother."

"No, no. I know I told you to call your mother. But I'm going to tell you, don't ever talk to your mother like that. You can't 'a'ight' her or dismiss her."

"She ain't have a problem with it."

"But I do, and I am a mother. So maybe she doesn't want to have that type of conversation with you, but I will. Don't you ever in your life, as long as I'm in your space, talk to your mother like that."

"A'ight. A'ight."

"Malik! What did I just say?"

Malik wasn't a bad kid or even a troublemaker; he was just always in trouble. It was heavy as he sat across from my desk and admitted he "always" failed, not least of all because this wasn't the first hard conversation he and I had had that week.

Two days earlier, I had let him know he wasn't going on the big Harvard trip with the rest of the school. In a much-publicized event, people from all over the world had funded the trip once they learned that there was a principal who wanted her underserved students to experience what it was like at one of America's elite institutions of higher learning. Everyone at Mott Hall was excited beyond words to go, but Malik and a handful of other students wouldn't be invited to participate. He wasn't going because of his defiance toward adults, although he tried to argue, "I can act right on a trip."

"First," I told him, "you have to remember that acting right starts in school. If you don't behave yourself here and respect the adults who love you, then you don't get the privilege of choosing when it will be convenient for you to do so. I don't prepare you for trips. I prepare you for life," I said. "You need to identify how we can help you become the best scholar. Because if you think the only way of surviving life is going on a Harvard trip, then your priorities are not in the right place."

Now that he had come into my office to explain the source of his attitude and anger, I knew it was genuine. He wasn't trying to ingratiate himself, because Malik and all the kids at Mott Hall knew me better than that. My expectations are high and I never waver from them. He wasn't going on the trip, which hadn't been an easy decision for me. I didn't enter education to punish children.

In the last few days, though, something in Malik had clicked, a nebulous connection between attitude, trust, and opportunity. He was in my office to finally talk about what was keeping him from succeeding in school. This was a moment of great achievement, at least in my school.

By all accounts—economic, social, academic—the state of education in America for children of color living in disadvantaged communities is extremely poor, while the consequences for them if they don't make it in school are severe. Many issues contribute to the devastating difference between education for white children and education for those of color, including poverty, inequitable distribution of resources, and lower parental involvement and education levels. But the punitive way the system deals with children of color can't be underestimated.

The so-called school-to-prison pipeline starts early. According to the latest numbers available from the U.S. Department of Education's Civil Rights Data Collection, black students, who represented 18 percent of preschoolers between 2011 and 2012, made up 48 percent of preschool students who received more than one suspension. Compare that to white students, comprising 43 percent of all preschool students, who made up only 23 percent of the suspensions—in other words, children of color are suspended at twice the rate of white children in *preschool*. That's just the start. Nationwide, black students—whose teachers on the whole have less experience and are paid less than those in majority-white schools—are suspended or expelled at three times the rate of white ones.

Integration has proven in study after study to offer the best outcomes in terms of bringing up test scores for children of color. But after the initial commitment to desegregation through court orders and thirty-five years of enforcement of the 1954 *Brown v. Board of Education* decision, around 1989, schools began reverting to levels of segregation not seen since the sixties. There are a number of reasons that this is so, including the fact that many federal agencies no longer take an active role in enforcement of integration. The proportion of black students in schools with a majority of white students, 23.2 percent, was lower in 2011 that it was in 1968.

Today's answer to the problems of students who aren't learning has been to create higher standards under the rubric Common Core, a blanket measure against which all schools nationwide—impoverished or wealthy—are judged. The other solution is to offer school choice, by way of charter schools, where public money goes to schools that don't have to follow public school guidelines. There are all kinds of charters, but the innovation that most of them feature focuses on high test scores as the only measure of success.

In that context, Mott Hall is a different kind of place. First of all, we're not a charter school (which I'll explain in more detail later). My goal for my students, who are primarily economically disadvantaged and of color, is twofold. First, in the short time that I have them, I want them to be what they are—children—and second, I want to give them the skills to be confident as students when they leave. I want them to play, learn, build resiliency, take risks, become compassionate—all without worry about failure. I'm hard on the adults in this building, because there are no second chances with our children.

Once they leave us, few people will ever pour into them the love and belief in their abilities that we do. *Those* are high stakes.

Disheartening circumstances in no way reduce my expectations for excellence from my students. We have many inspirational sayings at our school, but one of my favorites is the name we've given to our kids: Brownsville Brilliance. This title turns the perceptions about them and their community on their heads. When I ask the scholars what the word *brilliance* makes them think of, they answer "intelligence," "radiance," and "diamonds." Yes, and what are diamonds but precious gems created when a large amount of pressure and force is exerted, just as it is on my scholars in life. In this way, we speak into existence how we find the positive in a place that has been discarded.

I, and the rest of the staff at Mott Hall Bridges Academy, who have committed to working with the most challenging communities, understand that, just as it takes a long time for carbon to become a diamond, change for our students is not an event, it is a process.

So when Malik, a boy who has to be defiant to survive on the streets of Brownsville, was able to make himself vulnerable enough to admit to me he was having trouble, yes, that was a big achievement.

I came around my desk and sat down next to Malik.

"One, I want to thank you for coming into my office

and admitting you're struggling. That is half the battle," I said. "What are you doing next week for spring break?"

"Nothing."

"You can come to school. I'll be here anyway, and I will sit with you and go through your work. Bring your books, so I can see exactly where you are struggling. You become angry and give attitude because you don't understand. Yes or no?"

"Yes."

"Then you need to promise me something. Use your words and let the adults know how we can help you. Got it?"

"Yes."

"Okay, then we're going to get through this together."

The
BRIDGE to
BRILLIANCE

CHAPTER ONE

THE VISION

I t's hard to imagine what it was like during the summer of 2010, the hottest on record, when I set out to find kids for a new middle school I was opening that fall in the Brownsville section of Brooklyn.

One of the poorest and most dangerous neighborhoods in all of New York City, Brownsville spans about two square miles made up mostly of housing projects. It doesn't matter which complex you're in—Brownsville Houses, Van Dyke Houses, Langston Hughes Houses, or Seth Low Houses—everybody knows who belongs and who doesn't. Residents eyed me suspiciously while I walked through the confusing mazes of bleak brick buildings in a simple button-down and capris. The glare from the sun off the concrete was so bright that I was blinded, but I didn't wear sunglasses because you have to see a person's eyes to trust them.

The seasoned vets hanging out on benches outside the playgrounds and apartment buildings gave me a look that said, "Who are you and why are you here?" The suspicion of these folks was palpable. And who could blame them? With their constant wail of sirens, massive floodlights, and unpopulated playgrounds enclosed by high fences, the projects felt more like prisons than places where people lived.

That summer the residents of Brownsville had been rocked by a spike in crime unprecedented even for the area. The stats were so shocking that they made the news. During a period of fifteen days in July, eleven people were shot, including a beloved fifteen-year-old boy named Ty-quan Jamison, who was killed while playing basketball by a gunman aiming for someone else. The wave of violence was attributed to the heat, but as I hit the streets, I could see clearly there were a lot of issues plaguing the neighborhood.

Looking for families, I introduced myself to anyone who would stop to listen. "Hi, my name is Nadia Lopez," I said. "I'm a principal opening up a school nearby called Mott Hall Bridges Academy."

My journey had begun five months earlier, when the New York City Department of Education (DOE) approved a proposal I submitted for a small middle school that would start with eighty sixth-grade students its first year, growing by a grade each year until Mott Hall Bridges reached its full scope, of roughly two hundred students in grades six through eight, by its third year.

I had been spurred on by the push for school choice put forth by Mayor Michael Bloomberg and his schools chancellor, Joel Klein. During the Bloomberg administration, 656 new schools opened up throughout the five boroughs that make up New York City (Manhattan, Brooklyn, Queens, Staten Island, and the Bronx). While 150 of them were charter schools (which receive public money but are not regulated by the policies of the New York City Department of Education), the vast majority were new district schools, usually colocated in empty or underutilized DOE buildings—just like Mott Hall Bridges Academy.

In 2008 I had first submitted the application for Mott Hall as part of the New School Process, a rigorous and competitive vetting procedure in which hundreds of candidates put forth proposals in the hope of getting an interview. I made the cut and presented before administrators from the Department of Education who asked questions about everything from the school's academic focus and its use of technology to its plan to get parents more involved.

The concept for my school was based on Mott Hall schools, a series of small schools throughout New York City focused on science, technology, engineering, and math (STEM). It fit the profile favored by the mayor, who was a strong proponent of small, thematic schools that draw on partnerships to support student success. My proposal was specifically modeled after a Mott Hall middle school in the Ocean Hill section of Brownsville, which I had chosen to replicate because of my close relationship with its principal, La Juan White. As a result, I spent a lot of time in its classrooms and offices. Although our curriculum was the same as that of all New York City public schools, we would have an additional focus on science and tech through an inquiry-based approach to learning and special electives, like robotics. I also adopted aspects of the culture in Ocean Hill's Mott Hall—such as uniforms and a formal code of excellence.

I heard back from the committee a month later; I didn't get my school. Naturally I was disappointed, but I was also grateful. I felt like I needed more time to hone my skills and get experience in an administrative position before I took on the responsibility of opening a brand-new school. I accepted a position as an assistant principal in a K–8 grade school in Ocean Hill. Ironically, one year later the DOE contacted me; they wanted me to consider opening my school in Brownsville, the community where I was currently serving. Now I felt I was fully up to the task and said yes.

Housed on the third floor of an already existing K–8 public school on Chester Street, Mott Hall Bridges Academy would be a district school that would have its own distinct culture and practices. But unlike charter schools, some of which Mayor Bloomberg also approved for colocation in larger public school buildings, my school would fall under the New York City schools chancellor and DOE policies.

Charter schools, which are governed by their own boards, set up their own policies and procedures on everything from discipline and curriculum to hiring practices. So, for example, they aren't under union contracts and therefore have the power to remove any staff member deemed unfit or incapable in terms of job performance. Or if a child doesn't meet the disciplinary standards, he or she can be expelled—and referred back to the district schools. District schools have to go through a lengthy process with the Department of Education to remove either a student or a teacher.

The other major difference between charter schools and district schools is in fund-raising and budget allocation. As nonprofit entities, charters can raise funds through private donations or other sources, and use the money in any way they deem fit. As a district school, we can't fund-raise unless we have a separate entity, like a parent-teacher association, with its own bank account and nonprofit status. Our funding is specifically from city, state, and federal sources. Any additional money we get, typically from grants, is managed by the public school funds. We have to submit a work scope order, detailing exactly what we want to use the money for and by what date we'll use it, in order to get the funding.

As soon as I received the news that my school could

open, in January 2010, I set to work on all the million and one things that needed to get done before the start of the school year that fall. One thing I didn't worry about was recruiting students, because the DOE's original plan was for me to fill my classes with eighty-four students from a neighboring school being phased out as a result of its failed ratings. However, that plan was thwarted when the NAACP asked the courts for an injunction against the closing. The courts eventually ruled in favor of the NAACP, the school stayed open, and I wound up with only eight students on my roster! I was forced to begin recruiting on June 26—the day after the school year ended.

That left me nearly no time to find a crop of sixth graders whose families were willing to take a chance on an unfamiliar face and school. But opening a school was a dream come true for me, and I would do whatever it took to find my kids. So I hit Sutter and Rockaway Avenues, Mother Gaston Boulevard, anywhere I thought I could catch parents. I attended community events and hung out at Betsy Head Park. I even set up a cupcake stand on the corner of Blake and Rockaway, trying to entice prospective candidates. *Anyone*—I mean anyone—who had a child going into sixth grade could sign up.

Armed with official materials from the DOE so people would understand this wasn't some type of scam, I presented myself with the professionalism of a principal and the warmth of a parent, which I knew from my experience was the key ingredient in getting parents to respond. Still, a lot of people wouldn't even stop to talk to me. Maybe some thought I was a fraud, but the majority were jaded by their experience with the school system. The previous DOE administration had done a lousy job of explaining to the community why they were opening new schools instead of fixing the ones that existed. Parents were not part of the process and therefore felt decisions were being imposed upon them. People in the neighborhood were angry that no one ever asked *them* what they needed.

The instinct to become territorial was natural. From what I could see, it wasn't like the outsiders who had come before had done such great things for the community. Why should they trust me? They didn't know me—and I didn't know much about them. Even though I was born and raised in Brooklyn, Brownsville was that place you never ventured into. When my mom, a nurse's assistant, worked in the area at Brookdale Hospital, she would always tell me stories about the robberies on Pitkin Avenue and the neighborhood's generally bad reputation for drugs and violence. Our neighborhood, Crown Heights, wasn't exactly Park Avenue. Comparatively, though, Brownsville was too dangerous a place to be.

It was years after my mom left her job at Brookdale that I went to work in Brownsville as an assistant principal at P.S. 73. Although I only spent a year in the position before receiving the call to open up Mott Hall Bridges, my experience there was so difficult that when I heard my new school was going to be located in the heart of Brownsville, I had to think hard about what I was getting myself into.

It's not that I was afraid of a challenge. When I had decided to make a career change in 2003, leaving Verizon, where I had worked in accounts receivable for four years (and giving up a third of my salary) to become a teacher, I had a one-year-old daughter and a marriage that was on the rocks (and ultimately failed). Still, I knew joining NYC Teaching Fellows, an alternative certification program, was what I wanted to do. The fellows program, created in 2000 in response to the worst teacher shortage New York's public school system had experienced in decades, helped fast-track people into the profession through training, subsidizing master's programs, and finding positions in schools. Through the program I was placed as a special education teacher at Dr. Susan S. McKinney Secondary School—a sixth- through twelfth-grade school in Fort Greene full of hurt, underprivileged children. At McKinney, where I spent three years, I was moved by the power of education to transform even the most hardened students. The experience wasn't unique to McKinney. In my next position, at the Urban Assembly Institute of Math and Science for Young Women, a girls' school I joined as a founding teacher in 2006, again I discovered how much children could change and grow if they were only given the chance.

It wasn't until 2008, though, while I was attending New Leaders—a highly acclaimed yearlong residency program dedicated to developing effective educational leaders and policies—that my thinking about education crystallized. Periodically the residents gathered for national seminars, where top professionals in the field inspired us with talks on their areas of expertise. We learned about everything from data-driven instruction to democratic classrooms, often from the people who literally wrote the book on the subject. But it wasn't just exposure to the cream of the crop in education that inspired and focused me. Surrounded by like-minded peers, those who believed that every kid could learn and that, despite the adversities, we had the capability to make that possible, I knew exactly the kind of school I wanted to lead.

So when my proposal for a middle school was accepted, I didn't know who the teachers or students were going to be (or where I was going to find the furniture). But I already had a clear vision that it was going to be a clean space with lots of activities and electives so that the students would know they had options. And it was going to be a place where the children loved learning. But mostly it was going to be a school whose kids knew they could take over the world.

That concept was part of what inspired the school's

name. Mott Hall is the name of the group of public schools on which I based the model for mine, but Bridges was about something way more personal.

During my first year of teaching at the middle school in Fort Greene, I was lucky to be paired with an incredible coteacher, Ms. DeCoteau. She not only helped me get through that first year at McKinney, where I taught seventh-grade special education social studies, despite the fact that my background was in science. Ms. DeCoteau also took me on her students' annual walk over Brooklyn Bridge.

Even though they lived less than a mile away from the Brooklyn Bridge, most of the kids in our class hadn't even seen it, let alone walked over it. As we started up the long approach from Tillary Street, getting closer to the granite towers of the iconic bridge with every step, the kids got so scared. By the time we were in the middle of the bridge— the thick suspension cables on either side of us, the East River and rushing cars below, and the Manhattan skyline in front—a few of the students were clutching me. The kids who were the most scared on the Brooklyn Bridge were the same ones who had reputations for being physically aggressive toward their peers or cursing out adults.

"What's wrong with you?" I asked Jayla, a small girl who made her clothes and had a real talent for it but was always fighting.

"Is the bridge going to fall?" she asked.

"Are you serious?" I said, but looking into her eyes I could see she was dead serious. "No, it's not going to fall. You're going to be okay. Just stay close to me."

I held on to Jayla, Sean, Darius, Anthony, and Imani, all kids I had so many problems with during the school year, and together we got over the bridge just like I promised.

Once on the Manhattan side, we walked to the South Street Seaport, where the kids I thought I knew so well surprised me again. These seventh graders, usually so rambunctious it was hard for them to learn, sat completely still on benches beside the pier. They were mesmerized by the water.

For an hour they sat there—kids who yelled at the top of their lungs in the hallways of school—not moving, not bothering anybody, not taking their eyes off the water and boats. They had never seen anything like it. And neither had I. I found the image of those kids just looking out at the water so inspiring and heartbreaking that I took a picture.

In that moment I realized the power of going places. These kids, so full of swagger in their little corner of the universe, were awed by the smallest taste of what was outside the walls of their projects and school. Some might say, "Well, what about their parents? Why don't they take their children places?" I'm sure my students' parents didn't have anyone taking them to see things around the city either, and anyway, blaming parents can't be the excuse for not exposing children to a variety of places and experiences. I can tell you this: nobody wants to feel like they are less than anyone else.

So when I thought about my new school, I knew that walking over the Brooklyn Bridge would be a rite of passage for us all. To my future students, I would say, "The bridge represents our past, present, and future. We're going to walk together so that you know you should never be fearful of anything or ever limit yourself. Whether it's new heights or new places, I got you. We'll hold hands and get through it, because if we're connected we will succeed. Then you can say, 'I made it,' and know you can make it anywhere."

The bridge didn't just pay homage to Brooklyn, my hometown; it also signified movement and evolution. I watched how the physical act of walking across the Brooklyn Bridge was also a powerful mental experience for my students at McKinney. As they moved out of the confines of the Ingersoll and Walt Whitman Houses to a wide-open skyline, their view of what was beyond their neighborhood was instantly expanded. It was a metaphor for the transition I wanted my students to go through as they entered in sixth grade and graduated in eighth. My school would be the bridge from the past and the place they came from to the future and a better place they were headed.

Out of that I named the school Mott Hall Bridges Academy and created our motto, "Connected to Succeed." It was important to me that the school have a name and not a number, like P.S. 132 or I.S. 58, because I felt that too often children in underserved communities such as Brownsville are defined by numbers—and not for the good. Numbers on state exams define whether or not they are smart enough to succeed, and the answer is usually a resounding *no*. If they are incarcerated, the criminal justice system takes away their names and replaces them with numbers.

In the short amount of time I had spent at P.S. 73 in Brownsville, I was struck by the fact that there was nothing in these kids' lives that validated their intelligence or encouraged them to believe they could elevate themselves out of the circumstances in which they were born. The system kept telling them that they were failing. But the way I saw it, the system was failing them.

The elementary school built into one of the housing projects is adjacent to a firehouse, so little children trying to learn are interrupted all day by screaming sirens. While I was at the Advanced Leadership Institute, a program through the Department of Education in collaboration with Baruch College, I did a study on the structural inequities of District 23, which comprises the neighborhoods of Brownsville, Ocean Hill, and parts of East New York, by comparing it to District 13, covering parts of Brooklyn Heights, Fort Greene, and other neighborhoods that have been gentrified like most of the borough. What I discovered was even more upsetting than I had anticipated. District 23 has only one traditional ninth- through twelfth-grade high school (whereas District 13 has eleven), evidence that there is a lack of belief that the children who live here will make it to high school.

Whether it's that the press keeps calling their home the murder capital of New York or that money is constantly being taken away from their school budgets, when these students face so many reminders that they aren't worth an investment, they start to believe it.

I kept this in mind with every decision I made before the opening of Mott Hall Bridges. One of those decisions was what the colors of the school should be. This wasn't an insignificant detail. Part of creating community and a proud space would be having a unified décor and dress code that reminded everyone of our mission. But what colors? Burgundy and khaki were already being used, and I can't stand black and white because of my own memories of assembly in elementary school. Green just didn't stand out . . .

Inspiration struck at an African doll show I attended with Miss Debbie—the mom of a friend from my own middle school days who collected handmade black dolls. While I was looking over all the little figures in various costumes, I homed in on a picture of a doll with a little headdress sitting atop her curly hair. "Oh, look at her!" I said.

"Do you realize you keep picking up everything that's

purple?" Miss Debbie asked. "Purple is the color of royalty. So this little lady symbolizes future African queens."

"Yeah, that she does," I said.

I continued to look at the picture, and that's when it hit me. "Purple," I said. "The school colors are going to be purple and black, because my students are going to be little queens and little kings."

And that's how I got the colors for Mott Hall Bridges, because I wanted everything to remind my children that they *were* kings and queens, or at least important. I could have even addressed them as royalty: "Good morning, King. Good morning, Queen." And I considered it, but I wanted a term that was gender neutral, so that when I was having a conversation with the entire school, I didn't have to rhetorically split the boys from the girls. So I settled on *scholars,* because in my mind it has the dignity of royalty but with the added connotation of lifelong learners.

All these details were crucial to me because I believe education is not just about academics. If you are going to save lives, you have to give children the right spaces, resources, cues, and support for them to share, figure themselves out, and then learn.

This remained my vision as a muggy July turned into an unbearable August. I had big dreams and even bigger goals; meanwhile, I didn't even have a copy machine. More important, I still didn't have enough scholars to fill one classroom.

Just as children wouldn't take learning seriously unless their teachers and principal proved that there was a reason for them to do just that, I knew that parents wouldn't buy into Mott Hall Bridges unless they saw me as someone who honored and respected their space. It wasn't enough to declare that I was a principal with a vision; I had to immerse myself in the community. Because they thought I was either bold enough to walk through their projects or crazy enough to show up to anything, including the annual neighborhood event known as Old-Timers Day, I became known throughout the community. I had to engage every single person—saying over and over like a broken record, "I need kids."

But when I finally held a formal informational meeting at the school—and only six parents showed up—it didn't seem like there was anything I could do to counter the problems of the past. There was nothing concrete in place to help people envision what our success could look like except my relentless insistence that every child who went through Mott Hall was destined for greatness and that a quality education was his or her birthright. Despite the small group in front of me, I gave my official presentation with as much energy and enthusiasm as I could. When I was done, the one male in the group approached me.

"Oh, I *had* to meet the woman who walked through the projects," he said, putting out his hand.

The man turned out to be Aliyah's father. I had met

Aliyah's mother a few weeks earlier while walking through the Seth Low Houses (where at one point a pair of cops asked me if I was okay). She had been sitting on a park bench with her daughter while I was attempting to give out flyers and introduce myself to prospective parents. She and I got into a conversation about how she hadn't let her daughter out of her sight ever since a recent shootout in one of the housing developments, where a bullet nearly struck her daughter. "Aliyah, tell her," she said to her.

"She doesn't let me go anywhere," the girl said.

I looked her mom straight in the eye and vowed, "Your daughter will not only be safe in my school but she'll learn. We will give her opportunities to go beyond Brownsville."

Aliyah's mother didn't respond either way at that moment, but Aliyah's dad made their feelings about my efforts very clear at the meeting: "When her mama told me about you, I said, 'Oh yeah, *this* is the school for us.'"

In the end, though, Ms. Hernandez, another mom who attended my open house, was the very first parent to officially enroll her daughter, Maria, at Mott Hall. She was a character, a small and very serious woman whom I could feel sizing me up while I gave my pitch for the school. But at the end of it she said, "Yup, sign me up. I'm having my daughter come to this school."

I was thrilled. My first customer.

"Could you do me a favor, Ms. Hernandez, and let other parents know about this school?" I asked.

"Absolutely not," she said, completely surprising me. "My daughter, Maria, is special. For too long, I've dealt with kids who don't want to learn. I don't want my daughter—who is a gift—to be distracted by anybody else's child."

I realized then and there that the parents of Brownsville, like Ms. Hernandez, were no different from parents anywhere else; they simply want the best for their children. Still, I couldn't open Mott Hall if Maria was the only student enrolled, which I explained to Ms. Hernandez as I asked her to spread the word and vouch for me.

After giving me a good hard look, she said, "I'll think about it."

CHAPTER TWO

THE TEACHERS

On September 8, 2010, Mott Hall Bridges opened with twenty-four sixth graders—way fewer students than the original goal, but a miraculous number considering the obstacles. That number rose to forty-five within the month as the Office of Enrollment sent us anyone who moved into the district after the start of school or for some reason couldn't be handled anywhere else.

Despite my campaign throughout the summer to convince families of Mott Hall's mission, our kids didn't really come from families buying into what we were offering. Instead we got children who had just arrived in the country or who required a different setting because they were known to do things like choke someone until that person's eyes rolled back. There was an assumption that because we were a small school, we could manage kids with severe behavior issues. But the reality was that we were new and our teachers were for the most part inexperienced.

Every single one of those forty-five children recited the Mott Hall Bridges pledge, which I created as another way for them to understand the value of the space they were in and ally themselves with it.

> We are the Mott Hall Bridges Scholars, we pledge to:
>   Respect ourselves, our peers, and the adults in
>   our community;
>   Practice kindness to those around us;
>   Show enthusiasm for the opportunities ahead
>   of us;
>   Strive toward exemplary achievement in all
>   that we do;
>   Practice good citizenship, and work hard to be
>   the best scholars we can be.

Despite their taking the pledge and my posting it on the walls of the school, from day one, the scholars were unruly and it was crazy. *Crazy.* There is no other word for what went on in those halls that first year. Kids screamed at the top of their lungs or walked out of rooms in the middle of class; it felt like an asylum rather than a school. My staff and I would routinely receive threats and get cursed out by parents when we called home in relentless efforts to hold them accountable for their children. It was no wonder my scholars were so mean to one another. Every single day there was a fight. Every single day. It wasn't unusual for me to spend at least two hours in my office with a group of children who had been tearing each other's hair out or otherwise demeaning one another. When they set fire to the bathroom, by burning toilet paper, I didn't think it could get any more insane.

Opening up Mott Hall Bridges was, by far, the biggest challenge I had ever faced. The obstacles I had to overcome had started way before a single scholar walked through the school doors. They ranged from the mundane (my office was an old science lab with the original equipment still in place, and we didn't get furniture or supplies until the first day of school) to the major (the NAACP lawsuit that impeded us from absorbing students from a school that should have closed, making our student count low). The Department of Education took $250,000 from my original budget because of the low enrollment, which meant I couldn't afford a guidance counselor or an assistant principal (I became both). I had a small number of scholars, but they had tremendous needs. Mott Hall Bridges is 98 percent African American and Latino, and it has almost the same percentage of children eligible for free or reduced-price lunch (the official stats say the lunch eligibility is only 75 percent, but many of the kids don't turn in their forms). On top of that, roughly 30 percent of my kids have been diagnosed with some form of disability that requires an individualized education plan.

The upshot of all this was that the five teachers and two staff members who made up my first team had to take on even more than all I had expected of them when they were hired.

In my original vision of Mott Hall—scholars in purple and black, loving learning and owning their futures—a big part of the picture was the teachers. I imagined when our kids were asked what they loved about their school, they would say, "We had the best teachers." And what did that mean? People who listened to them, adults who really cared.

I knew firsthand the crucial role teachers and others who work in schools play in the lives of children, not just intellectually but also emotionally.

My own middle school years had been tough ones. It began when I was in seventh grade and had just gotten back from a school trip to Hershey Park. My mom and I were on the B25 bus in Brooklyn, riding home when she dropped the bombshell. "Things are going to be a little different when you get home," she said quietly. "Your dad, he's not going to be there anymore."

I didn't understand what she was saying. My mom, a nurse's aide originally from Guatemala, and my dad, a native of Honduras who worked as a photographer, had met at a party in the Bronx. I, their only child, had never seen my parents argue and had no idea there were any issues between them. Did she mean just for today? I couldn't imagine life at home without him. Ever since I was little I was a daddy's girl: tagging along with him on his photography assignments and learning how to take apart and repair simple electronics just like he did.

But a few days later, when I woke in the morning, my dad and his friend were moving all his stuff out of the apartment. When he came into my room, I pretended I was still sleeping so I didn't have to say good-bye. When I went to school, I acted like nothing had happened—except that when the day was over, instead of going home, I went to the administrative office, where the school coordinator, Paula Holmes, worked. An experienced educator, she didn't have to ask me any questions but instinctively knew I needed to be in that space. I stayed at school until eight o'clock that night.

For the next two years, until I graduated from middle school, Ms. Holmes let me stay in the building late every single day. When I was done with my homework, I did office work. I learned to file and to use the computer. For me, school was a refuge, because that was where I didn't have to feel the pain of the struggles of home. I didn't have to explain myself, and no one had to feel sorry for me. Everything I needed was there.

Of course, sweeping your feelings under the rug is not a long-term solution. Through the rest of middle school and into high school, I missed my dad and was mad at my mother that he wasn't with us. I didn't understand what was happening at home, but I never said anything to my mom about my feelings. I also never talked about what was happening to anyone else because the rule was: what happens in our home stays in our home.

When my repressed emotions began to bubble up in detrimental ways, again it was an educator who came to my rescue. During my junior year at A. Philip Randolph Campus High School in Harlem, I found myself failing every class. I felt suffocated at home. My mom was getting on my nerves all the time. We didn't communicate or have anything in common. I was so unhappy that I stopped applying myself at school. I thought nobody was paying attention, but I turned out to be wrong. One day my history teacher, Mr. Pearson, called me over to ask, "What's going on with you?"

Mr. Pearson—an avid gun collector, basketball fan, and amazing storyteller—was my favorite teacher, because his class was always interesting and personal. He had us do things like debate the various conspiracy theories about the Kennedy assassination (he thought two gunshots from one person was impossible), and he always connected everything we learned in class back to his family.

"Things aren't good at home," I confessed to him. "It's stuff going on that I would really rather not talk about."

Mr. Pearson, who was so cool, didn't press me. But the simple act of him asking me what was going on, letting me know someone saw me and cared, was enough to help. It wasn't long after that that I decided on my own to go see the social worker (her office was near Mr. Pearson's classroom, which I think made it easier for me to drop by). During our counseling sessions, I was able to talk about what I had kept bottled up for so long, how I had spent so much time and energy trying to protect my mother that I no longer felt like putting effort into anything.

Life got better, and so did my grades. Having conversations about problems with people who care always helps. So when I posted ads for teachers at Mott Hall in the summer of 2010, I knew just how important these people would be. My dream was to find teachers who were optimistic and took ownership of their roles. I wanted them to experience something similar to what the scholars would, that through this school they were going to change the world.

The challenge, though, was that no one wanted to come to Brownsville, and definitely not to a school without a track record of success or kids on a roster. Although I posted ads on Web sites like Craigslist and Idealist, attended hiring fairs for teachers held at the Brooklyn Museum, and spread the word among educators I knew, I didn't get a lot of applicants, and out of those, even fewer viable ones.

The majority of people who submitted résumés that first year fit into three basic types. There were those who were overqualified for the jobs I had posted—veterans with administrative experience and so much on their applications that it was more than likely they wanted to use a new school in a tough neighborhood as a quick stepping-stone into a leadership role. I wanted people who were willing to grow with the program—plus I could never have afforded those veteran salaries on my lean budget. Then there were the folks who had gotten "unsatisfactory" on their observations and annual ratings year after year. I might not have had a lot of options, but there was no way Mott Hall Bridges was going to become a dumping ground for failed teachers. Last, there were the newbies who, simply put, didn't have any experience with a high-needs community.

Thank God I had Ms. Achu by my side during the disheartening hiring process. I had met the tall, spunky Texas native at the Urban Assembly Institute of Math and Science for Young Women, where the coprincipals empowered staff like Ms. Achu and me to develop our own programming, take our students on field trips, and develop the art of building strong partnerships. Ms. Achu, who had graduated from Southern Methodist University before earning a master's degree at Boston University, proved that she was more than smart. Her passion for helping the girls was evident. Ms. Achu was firm, disciplined, consistent, and loving. I knew we'd need all those qualities in Brownsville if we were going to survive.

That's why one of the first things I did when I learned the DOE had approved my application for Mott Hall was to call Ms. Achu. "I won't open this school without you," I said. She made me wait three days but finally agreed to join me. I breathed a sigh of relief and made her my director of programs.

I got lucky that Mr. Principal and Mr. Martinez, two teachers from P.S. 73 in Brownsville, where I had been assistant principal, were looking for a new challenge. While I was at P.S. 73, I had admired the way Mr. Principal moved kids' scores up in his math classes. When I asked him why he was willing to join my experiment at Mott Hall, he said, "Whether or not I agree with you, Lopez, I always understand what you want and what it will take to get there. You are very clear about your goals and help figure out the steps needed to achieve them." That was good enough for me.

Mr. Martinez, meanwhile, became the school's dean. I also found a teacher for humanities (a combination of social studies and English language arts, or ELA) enthusiastic about our mission at Mott Hall, who seemed like a perfect fit.

I was still looking for my science and special education teachers when July turned into August. That's when I really began to worry, because even the staff I'd already hired wouldn't have enough time to plan before the start of school. One of the biggest mistakes teachers make is trying to teach material they haven't given themselves enough time to master. So I finally took a brand-new special education teacher, who e-mailed and called me all the time, which was a sign of either a high level of commitment or neediness. Only time would tell. My science teacher was brand-new as well, but Ms. Paul got the job because she was the only person who showed up. I hired a secretary, and like that we opened up a school.

Whenever you are starting something new, there is so much to do and to figure out. For our new teachers, who were still learning their craft, this added stress proved a heavy burden. But even for our more experienced staff, like Mr. Principal and Mr. Martinez, that first year at Mott Hall wasn't much easier. Not only were we a new school with all the difficulties that naturally come with being new, but we also lacked funding for necessities such as books and technology. The quarter of a million dollars I lost before we even opened meant that I had to make some quick decisions on budget cuts—they included losing intervention services for children who weren't reading on grade level as well as passing on using novels and workbooks in the classroom. We had *no* textbooks for the children; the teachers had to make do with handouts that they had prepared using the school's copy machine.

It wasn't a good solution, but I had no choice. In general, books are necessary to the work of teachers. For my group—facing an extremely challenging student body at a time when American schools were starting to transition to the whole new Common Core method of learning—not having the most basic tools of their craft was like being sent into battle without any armor.

My teachers were doing the best they could in the circumstances, and it was my job to make sure they had an outlet for their frustrations and support when they were struggling. That's why I have a true open-door policy—anyone can come in pretty much any time of the day, and I will put down what I'm doing and talk about what's going on. Mr. Principal dubbed me his "therapist" because of our countless conversations in my office. Our talks usually went the same way.

"These kids are just insane," he'd say. "I mean they are an insane group of individuals. Lighting toilet paper on fire. Why would you *want* to do that? I just don't get it."

"They are the way they are because no one thinks they should be better," I would reply. "Everything around them says they should be criminals, teenage moms, and just crazy. But they can and will be better."

"I don't know. I grew up in East Flatbush, where we had our share of knuckleheads, but it was different. What really frustrates me is their lack of desire to do better. I'm Haitian, and in my culture, school is everything. Here the attitude is 'I just don't care.'"

I wanted Mr. Principal to have the same faith I did—that our scholars could and would be better but just needed to be given the opportunity. I would have the same conversation as many times as it took to get him to share my belief.

"Not everyone who has a choice knows they have a choice," I said. "Why try if you feel like you don't matter? And when no one is able to protect you from gang or gun violence, hunger, or abuse, why should you think you matter? This is what they believe, even if it's not normal or right. Our job, the whole point of this school, is to give them a choice and bring some normalcy to their lives."

If I was asking my teachers at Mott Hall to carry the heavy burden of giving our children a choice, I had to be in it right with them. Yet we were a school, and fundamentally the scholars were there to become proficient academically, so it was my job to make sure that was happening—no matter the obstacles.

After the first month of school, during which I spent almost all my time just trying to get more students into the building, I started doing daily observations so that I could see for myself how the children were learning. Whenever I walked into a classroom, I greeted the teacher and then the scholars. I'm not a spy lurking in their room, taking notes with which to render a verdict later. Rather I'm a participant who wants to give everyone the respect they deserve, even or especially when I'm upset with them. If they don't respond to my reprimand or critique immediately, they still know that their opinions matter.

In the long run, I believe it's much more important to get everyone to work together than it is to win any particular battle.

Unfortunately, what I discovered as soon as I started to watch carefully was that my new teachers, thrown into this high-stress environment, were drowning. Ms. Paul, the science teacher, was inexperienced in managing a classroom, and it showed. She didn't know how to make lesson plans or engage the scholars, which meant kids, bored in her class, erupted in a fight every day. I had intimate knowledge of this behavior because her room was right next to my office.

Her problem was that she ran a teacher-centered environment: she talked too much and didn't interact with the children enough to draw them into the material. This was the perfect recipe for disaster because it created a setting in which scholars could verbally antagonize one another. It would start with "Why you looking at me?" "She shouldn't be looking at me!" And then, without thinking, they'd jump up and start fighting. (In that class it happened to be the girls beating up the boys.)

When I ran into the classroom to see what was going on, Ms. Paul was like a deer in headlights. Frozen and utterly silent, she watched her room descend into chaos. I didn't scream at the kids or yell at her about what was going on (as a principal, you have to model how you want others in your building to act). But I explained to the scholars that they were off task by reminding them of the expectations for them reinforced by the school's pledge, inspirational quotes on posters on all the school's walls, and even the school's mottos on their uniforms.

"I see a child who is wearing a T-shirt that says 'Scholar.' Are you embodying any of the qualities of a scholar?" I asked the kids, who had been acting up just a minute earlier.

"No," they said.

At Mott Hall we were charged with the huge task of instilling self-control in students who had never been challenged to prioritize their education, and we would never succeed in doing this without putting the ownership back on them. Getting them to take responsibility for their actions also served as a way to avoid shaming Ms. Paul, who had clearly lost control of her class.

After class, when I got Ms. Paul into my office to ask what had happened, she burst out crying. "I don't know," she said. "I tried to engage them, but . . . I don't know."

It was clear that my science teacher was having trouble. But she had a lot of heart. What had stood out for me during our interview—as she described deciding she wanted to work in the inner city after volunteering for a community-based nonprofit—was her commitment to those less fortunate. We just needed to work on her skills.

I came in on Saturdays to help her plan out her units, but it quickly became clear I couldn't give her the time she needed. So I hired a coach to sit in her classes, give her feedback, model-teach, and write lesson plans with her. It was hard to find the money in the budget, but I felt the expense of giving a new teacher the support she needed to grow was worth it. Still, it was money that could have been used on other things.

So I was frustrated when I later discovered that, even after their teacher had received extensive professional development, half the scholars in Ms. Paul's class were failing. When I asked why, her reply was "The kids are not doing the work." When many children aren't doing the work, there is a problem—and it typically has to do with the assignments. I asked her if she had given the scholars specific directives. No. Walked them through a model assignment? No. All the assumptions she had made in creating lesson plans that didn't engage a classroom were there in her assignments. But what aggravated me as we started from square one, writing together a series of performance tasks for the children to follow, was that she hadn't reflected on what she might have been doing wrong when so many scholars were failing to turn in the work.

Ms. Paul wasn't the only one on my teaching staff who was struggling. I was disappointed when the English teacher and the special education teacher, paired as a team, couldn't stand each other. Each was constantly in my office to complain about the other one, so I brought them in together to clear the air—because I believe in total transparency. Instead of trying to resolve the problem, they acted like they didn't know what I was talking about.

But my real problem with the English teacher came with the way she dealt with the scholars. In the beginning she had taught beyond her students' skill set, so, similar to Ms. Paul's students, the children didn't hand in their work and were rowdy. After sitting in on her class, I provided recommendations for material and modeled an approach that would build on what the scholars already knew.

Sitting in on her class on poetry analysis in the middle of the year, I couldn't believe the poem she had chosen to analyze—"Humpty Dumpty"! From teaching over their heads, she had swung wildly the other way, to completely underestimating them. The kids were snickering, and I didn't blame them. Was "Humpty Dumpty" even a poem? Then, instead of engaging them in a conversation about the intention, mood, and theme (if "Humpty Dumpty" had any of those things), she handed out work sheets for the scholars to fill out. I watched as the kids disconnected because she had given them way too long to complete the task. Bored, they started to do things that were inappropriate. I had identified the problems—two classic ones: low expectations and trouble controlling the space.

I asked her to see me at the end of the day, and when she walked into my office, I didn't waste any time. While I am very direct about where I think people need professional development, and while I know this can be uncomfortable for those on the receiving end, I always try to follow up with solutions and resources to help them improve. I don't just list problems and faults and then say, "Deal with it."

"Let's start with the poem you chose today," I said. "Some of what is happening is that the scholars don't feel like they are being challenged."

"Well, I tried to do Emily Dickinson with them and they didn't get it at all," she said.

"You have to manage your lessons at a level where they feel some success. But you are going back to elementary school material, which cues them to start acting like elementary students. That's when you get the behavioral problems that turn into safety issues."

"It was in the teacher's ELA manual, but I chose a bad source. It's my fault."

I could see the teacher was getting defensive.

"To ask for help doesn't mean you are failing. You are sitting there in the dark trying to figure out what's going wrong with your lesson plans. You can't work in isolation. I seek out models I can follow to tell me where I'm going wrong and help me do it right."

"I don't know what poem to do with them if Dickinson is too hard and 'Humpty Dumpty' is too easy."

I put my head in my hands and said, "Start with Langston Hughes."

The next day the English teacher called in sick. I can only assume it was because she was frustrated and hurt by my critique. To me, pulling someone aside to say "You can do better" is a sign of respect—not a reason to run.

I had learned the value of high expectations during my first year at McKinney from Ms. DeCoteau, my coteacher. In our seventh-grade class, we had kids who could hardly read when they started the year. But she kept her room stocked with everything from picture books typically reserved for elementary school students to above-grade-level chapter books. "You all are going to read something. I don't care what it is. You're going to read," she said. And they did. Every day each student read and wrote, because Ms. DeCoteau demanded it. I witnessed one girl, Shanelle, go from struggling to read a picture book about butterflies and to write a single sentence in September to reading August Wilson's *The Piano Lesson* and writing an eight-page paper narrative by February of the same academic year. And her progress kept going and going. It was all about having high expectations and continuously pushing the students to achieve them.

That's what I saw myself doing with my teachers—having high expectations and pushing them to achieve. In education there is an odd premise that only the kids are supposed to be growing. But I think of how so many of my teachers have grown during their time at Mott Hall, even the strongest. Mr. Principal is a perfect example. He was an experienced math teacher with a history, as I said, of improving test scores. Still, whenever I observed his class and found scholars not following, I asked him to go over the material with me one-on-one to improve his approach.

Math teachers tend to think very conceptually and can easily skip the reasoning the rest of us need to go through to make true sense of an idea. As a student, I always had a lot of trouble in math. It literally made me sweat, so I was the perfect test audience to make sure Mr. Principal could teach his lesson to *anyone*. And he was always a willing participant

When I had him go over the lesson on volume with me, I could tell what he was saying made perfect sense in his mind. "The volume of a rectangle is length times width times height," he said. Meanwhile, I was already sweating.

"I need you to explain it in a way that I will understand," I said.

He tried a couple more times, but they were all variations on stating the formula. I could tell Mr. Principal was getting frustrated, but better with me than with the scholars. I asked him to describe a real-life example. After thinking for a moment, he came up with a brilliant one: a fish tank. Instead of making volume an abstraction, he asked me a series of questions that took me through a visual exercise of pouring water into a tank. When it goes in, the water has no choice but to take the shape of the bottom of the tank, which is a rectangle. Or put in another way, the water covers the area of the rectangle, which the children knew from previous lessons as length multiplied by width. Then he asked me if I kept pouring in the water, where would it go? Would it go up? Yes. How much? As high as the tank. Okay, that's the height. So if you want to figure out exactly how much water is in the tank, how would you do it? I pictured water in the shape of the rectangle in layer after layer until it reached the top. So it was the area of the rectangle (length times width) multiplied by the height of the tank.

Now that I could connect the concepts to something concrete, I didn't need the formula to calculate the answer. You don't need to memorize a formula if you understand what it does. Now it was easier not only for me but also for Mr. Principal's scholars. One day, years after he started at Mott Hall, he said to me, "I am a billion times better math teacher than when I first met you." But it was only because he was willing to try and try again until he could make the worst math student (in this case, me) understand.

Everyone on this planet has her blind spots, and it's a leader's job to coax sight, for personal growth if nothing else. Ms. Achu is my right hand, my rock, the clearest thinker, and a person who can execute even my craziest plans. But as smart, hardworking, and capable as she is, I felt she needed to be willing to take greater risks in order to reap greater rewards. The opportunity came to encourage her to put herself out there when Ms. Achu complained that she was having trouble finding step competitions for the team she had started in our school. Step, or stepping—a type of dancing originally from Africa in which intricate rhythms are made through footsteps and claps—grew out of historically African American fraternities and sororities. Because of her passion for step, Ms. Achu had formed a serious team at Mott Hall called RoyalVision, which scholars had to audition for and write an essay to join. But no one else in Brownsville, especially not in middle school, was doing a step competition.

"Let's host one here at Mott Hall," I said.

As with many of my ideas, Ms. Achu did not hesitate because I believed in her, which helped her believe in herself. Although she worked incredibly hard and thought out every detail of the competition, on the day of the event she was very, very nervous. She worried about everything. Were the five teams that had registered going to show up, or would they have second thoughts about driving into Brownsville? Had she e-mailed enough people about the show? Were there going to be just two people in the audience? The answer was no; when the competition started, our auditorium, which holds four hundred people, was almost full with parents, scholars, and other children who had heard about the show. The event was an unmitigated success for the school and for Ms. Achu.

This idea of continually pushing to do better, both as

individuals and as a school, is the reason I use $55,000—the equivalent of a teacher's salary—out of my slim budget to bring in seven teaching artists from outside the school to run an elective program for one period a week, every Tuesday morning. While it means the scholars get to do activities they want to do, such as African drumming, chorus, videography, social entrepreneurship, jewelry making, and fashion design (a rare thing for them), the program's true purpose is to free up the teachers so that we have about an hour a week to focus on common planning and schoolwide professional development. When everyone is in the room listening to the same thing, there can be no excuses for not having gotten the message.

Anyone who knows me knows I don't sugarcoat (there simply isn't enough time in my day), and when I feel my teachers are not meeting the standards I expect of them, I use that period to have hard conversations—which is exactly what I did after receiving an appalling attendance record for my staff.

I walked around the room, silently handing out a printout that showed each staff member's number of absences as well as the total hours and minutes of lateness. The names were redacted, but teachers didn't need to see their names to know who they were and how they measured up against the rest. It was very, very uncomfortable, but this was part of those difficult conversations I have all the time. As a team of professionals, our numbers were atrocious: only two people had no latenesses, and three of them topped out at more than thirty!

I taped a big piece of white paper to one of the walls and pulled out my colored markers. I wanted to make a strong visual statement so they would have no choice but to see the impact all of this was having beyond themselves.

"How much do you all make? What's your salary?" I asked.

No one spoke up. I wrote in big red numbers: $50,000–$60,000.

"That's not including benefits," I continued. "And this is for an entire year, where you don't work for two months during the summer, holidays, and weekends. If you *do* have to work more than your scheduled contract, how much do you make in overtime?"

Silence.

I took out a blue pen and wrote: $41.92 an hour.

"Now I have another question for you all. How much are our children making, when they sit in the class, and you're trying to figure *you* out?"

Silence.

"And if you fail them in the time that they've been here, what's minimum wage?"

Silence.

"It's seven twenty-five an hour," I said.

I did a quick calculation—in orange—of $7.25 per hour x 40 hours a week x 52 weeks a year. The result was $15,080 a year, which I circled in black.

"So this is what our scholars can hope to make when we fail to provide them with the best education by not showing up. That is, if they are lucky enough to get full-time hours and never get sick. And you're making a salary that's three or four times that when you don't even have to work an entire year? And your contract says that your day is six hours and twenty minutes, but because you work at Mott Hall Bridges Academy, technically you only work four hours, and you get lunch, and two prep or professional periods a day? And you have the audacity to act like this is hard or too much?

"The only individuals who get the short end are our scholars. When they come in late, some people lock the door or ask for a late pass that would require a scholar to walk all the way down the hallway. Yet if you come late, you clock in and keep moving. Ironically, there is no leniency for children, who often don't understand the implications and whose parents don't understand either because they have never been employed. You get to earn a check despite your lateness or absence."

I knew what I was saying was incredibly harsh, but the stakes for our children were so high that being brutally honest for a few minutes seemed like a small price to pay for the adults charged with their well-being. They needed to take their role seriously.

"You have the power of choice," I said. "You chose to come here. The children, they don't have a choice. They have to be here."

Adults tend to hold kids to higher standards than they have for themselves, and teachers are no exception. This is a theme I return to over and over as a principal, because I see it over and over. We all take children to task for things we overlook in ourselves.

When I send out an informational e-mail to my staff every weekend with a respond receipt tag, not everyone confirms their receipt, and probably even fewer actually read the e-mail. But I'm going to be consistent and send out the e-mail anyway. I'll never forget when my grandmother passed away, a teacher who had heard the news from another teacher came into my office to say he had just heard and to express his condolences.

"That's interesting," I said "Because it was the first line of the e-mail I sent out to the staff last week."

As I said, I'm perfectly fine being brutally honest.

When my teachers get upset that kids didn't read the assignment they put in the homework packet, I remind them that they don't read the letters I send. And when teachers lock the doors to their rooms so that kids who are late miss even more crucial instructional time as they fetch a late pass, when the teacher could just mark it down on his attendance record, I ask, "What does it cost to give a child some grace?"

As harsh as these conversations can be, when I conduct them during our Tuesday meetings, they aren't gotcha moments but a collective reckoning. My speaking to the group allows people to reflect on their own behaviors without feeling singled out. And I *always* see shifts in the teachers' behavior afterward—whether it's submitting their work in advance of the deadline or having a little more patience with a challenging scholar—even if those shifts aren't immediate.

The profession of teaching is not for everyone—and teaching in Brownsville is for even fewer people. The kids are difficult, but they're supposed to be difficult. They have to work ten times harder than students in Brooklyn Heights, the Upper West Side, or Tribeca just to stay afloat, because they come without parental and societal support. That means my teachers also have to work ten times harder than teachers in more affluent neighborhoods. It's not fair, but it is reality.

I'm respectful of the union, but there's no way you can do this job from 8:00 A.M. to 3:00 P.M. Good teachers go beyond what's required in their contract and put in those extra hours, whether it's to read a book or an article, observe other people's practices, or analyze their own work. Great teachers aren't just willing, they *want* to go beyond.

This motivation feeds into my larger ethos that learning has to go beyond the classroom to be really meaningful. I always ask my teachers to think about how they can connect the outside world to their lessons in school. Can they bring in objects? Or have guests come to talk about their lives? Teaching is so much bigger than paper, pen, and a textbook; it's an experience, we hope it's an experience a child will never forget.

One of the exercises I did with my staff early in that first year (and that I do whenever I think they need to be reminded) was to get them thinking about a favorite teacher from their own educational experience, and what made that person stand out. They listed qualities and fond memories of teachers who were always present; made learning fun; created safe spaces; knew your name; knew when you didn't understand; knew enough to pull you aside when something was going on; made you feel like you were relevant in the classroom. After we completed the list, I asked them, "Are you being that person for your kids? And, if you're not, what things can you change and how can I support you in being that person?

"At Mott Hall we have a culture of adults who believe in students," I told my teachers. "Even though it's not easy because we serve a community that is constantly at a disadvantage, I know you all want to be and can be *that* person for our children."

In order for that to happen, teachers have to view their

jobs as far more than the time they spend at the black-board. I told my staff straight up, "If you're counting how many hours you're supposed to work and are more concerned about your check than you are about children, you gotta go. You just have to go."

I am confident in my demands, because I have never asked my staff to do anything I wouldn't do myself. They understand I will do whatever it takes to make sure these kids are successful, including being in the building until all hours. Mr. Principal was always trying to get me to leave school when he found me at my desk way into the night. "I have been through five school leaders," he said, "and I've never seen anyone spend so much time in the office. The energy you have, to stay so late and then come back at eight A.M., that is not normal."

Then most of my staff isn't normal either, because they put so many extra hours into this school. (As Mr. Principal, who was the school's union rep, put it, "There is some voodoo that Lopez does that gets you to do it.") Not everyone can or wants to work the way I do, but for those who share my drive, it's a comfort to see me still in my office after they've spent a very long day teaching, talking to kids, running a club, and grading. It's the knowledge that we are in this thing together.

During that first year of Mott Hall, I never took a break. As much as I loved my teachers, it wasn't for their benefit alone. There was just so much to do running a new school that I worked every weekend and holiday. I don't think there was a day that Ms. Achu and I left school before ten o'clock at night. Because I had to be hands-on in the classrooms and with scholars and their parents, I didn't get to the business of being a principal until around 6:00 P.M. every day, answering a mass of e-mails that ranged from Compliance asking if my kids had taken their vision tests to mandatory professional development seminars and data analysis sessions.

Sometimes it felt like every moment was a low moment. (Although a particularly low one came when I discovered the school secretary was rolling in an hour and a half late every day after a parent asked why no one ever answered the phone in the morning. Because I gave a first-period character education class to the entire student body each morning, I had no idea the secretary wasn't at work. It didn't help that our clocking-in system wasn't working because of a problem with the wiring. Even after we fixed that, the secretary never could make it to school before the first bell.)

There were so many gaps to fill, needs to meet, and anger to address that I didn't blame my teachers when they fell into hopelessness or negativity. But I also knew that the way we would have the most success with any child was to identify and discuss his particular strengths and difficulties and how to bridge those two poles. That's how you develop entry points into the best way to teach to that child. (That is another reason for the electives and after-school programs Mott Hall offers. When academics can be frustrating, especially now, with so much testing, I want our scholars to feel a sense of success in *something*.)

I took one Tuesday morning staff meeting to illustrate my point. I used as an example Jeremiah, a scholar whose academic struggles had caused much debate among my staff. A special education student, Jeremiah was in some general education classes, but he also had two paraprofessionals who spent one-on-one time with him in and out of his classes to provide additional academic support.

I began the exercise during the staff meeting by asking the general education teachers to describe Jeremiah to me, and wrote down everything they said on a big piece of paper on the wall in blue marker. Here was their list:

—writes very slowly
—difficulty synthesizing info
—challenges with unfamiliar content
—easily distracted
—struggles articulating the process
—never completes the task on time, rushes
—gets lost in group work
—lacks motivation
—decoding issues
—no stamina to read
—difficulty inferencing

—lacks retention of info

—difficulty connecting ideas

—confused with what he is being asked to do

—struggles with basic computation

—lacks patience

—moves at his own pace

—needs time to express himself

—lacks academic confidence

—distraction related to academic struggle

—if not encouraged has zero motivation

Then I asked his two paraprofessionals to describe the same student, and they wrote down their observations in orange on the same paper. Here was their list:

—neat handwriting

—eager to please

—loves verbal participation

—strong visual and tactile activities

—likes rewards

—helpful

—loves to volunteer

—loves to be a part of the solution

—loves when he recognizes new words

—loves praise

—loves to be asked about himself

—concerned about others

The lists stood in stark contrast to each other. Simply put: everything in blue was negative.

After doing this exercise, the teachers were able to see their biases. If they couldn't think of positive things to say about Jeremiah, how were they approaching him? If they couldn't figure out any of his strengths, how could they engage him in instruction, increase his motivation, identify when he didn't complete the task, and figure out how to make him less of a distraction to others?

There's no magic educational theory or new program that is going to make teaching a difficult child in a difficult place easy. It always comes down to the same things: approaching the material in another way, repeating, having patience, being present, and never giving up. I started a new piece of paper to write a list for *all* staff to follow with *all* students:

1. Have real relationships and get to know the scholars.
2. Provide special directions/differentiation of instruction.
3. Know the expectations.
4. Provide incentives for motivation.
5. Do not embarrass scholars or call out their behavior in front of the class.
6. Work as a team and use our special-needs support team as a resource.

In some ways, though, I knew my exercise was unfair. Yes, I wanted my teachers to see Jeremiah as a whole child and not simply as the scholar who couldn't grasp the math concepts or sit still in English. But our educational system is not set up for teaching, at least not in the way I want it to be. The dynamics make the teacher race against the clock to get through the curriculum. That's in juxta-position to the paraprofessionals, whose role is to focus on the child and know that child's strengths in order to support him or her in completing the work. (That's why I believe paraprofessionals—assistants without a teach ing license, typically undervalued in school settings— offer a unique perspective and a solution-oriented method to learning.)

I'm hard on my staff because I'm hard on everyone. I'm hard on my daughter. I'm hard on my mom. I'm especially hard on myself. That's just how I'm built. Still, I under-stand how that can become overwhelming and counter-productive. I had to learn the point between pushing and breaking, between asking people to be better and making them feel like they aren't good enough.

I was serious about not asking my staff to do anything I wouldn't do, and so just as I asked them to consider what they needed to do to grow as teachers, I asked the same question of myself as a leader. What biases did I bring to the job?

Out of the five teachers I hired for Mott Hall's first year, only two remained the next year. (To date, of the thirty staff members employed over the five years of the school's existence, I have had to transition out fifteen because they were not the right fit for this community.)

In a place like Brownsville, it's so easy to get caught up on the deficits—of children, teachers, parents, budgets, even principals. I myself had to remember the very same lesson I had given to my teachers: that in order to support people you need to find the positive and use that as the starting place for improvement. The truth is, when I look at my staff, I see people who are passionate and full of potential. But often they don't see me seeing them this way, because I am tough and am concerned about everything we are up against.

Teaching, a profession where you pour yourself into children, is emotional by nature. We all have our personal issues, dealing with parenthood, a spouse, or any of the normal ups and downs of life. It's so easy for that to bleed into the classroom. That is why I arrange for a professional counselor to come to the school once a week to have conversations about how to manage expectations and frustrations in the classroom. For the last five years, Mr. Jenkins has come to do one-on-one sessions or group meetings to address the social and emotional needs that can arise in our school community. It's my way of providing support for the teachers without intruding on their privacy. Through those discussions, they get to talk about what's going on in their personal lives and ultimately how to separate that from the children. When I find compassionate and talented teachers, I will do anything to help them succeed, no matter how much they struggle.

Our art teacher, Ms. Dorn, experienced serious culture shock when she first arrived at Mott Hall because in the charter school where she had worked previously, she hadn't had to deal with kids with tough behavioral issues. Her completely normal response was to retreat from the children. But that only made them more aggressive around her. I knew she was the right teacher for our kids, but when I talked to the scholars about why they behaved poorly in her class, they said they didn't like her because she wasn't "nice" to them. When I dug a little deeper to understand what they meant by "nice," I found the biggest complaint was that she didn't smile at them.

On a day when the kids were being especially defiant— yelling-at-the-top-of-their-lungs, setting-the-bathroom-on-fire defiant—Ms. Dorn came into my office and I could tell immediately she was just done. But there was no way I was losing her.

"No, you're not leaving this school," I said. "You're going to really love what you do; and you're going to love it with these children. You just have to smile. And you have to talk to them. And I don't mean during detention. Just talk to them in the hallways and after class. Then you'll enjoy your job, and they'll enjoy you."

It's easy for a principal to say things like that, like a mom telling a hurting child, "Don't worry, everything will be fine." I had to find practical tools to bring her and the kids together. I asked Ms. Dorn what she liked to do in her spare time and found out that she is a beekeeper; she sells the honey from her hives; and she also sews. In fact, she said, she'd made the dress that she wore to her interview for Mott Hall. So I suggested she might do a sewing class with the scholars. Ms. Dorn said she'd also like to try beekeeping. "Go for it," I said.

I gave her every resource I could, but Ms. Dorn also hustled to make those classes happen in a high-level way. I couldn't believe it when I saw all the sewing machines she got for the school. She had some donated, paid for some out of her own pocket, and even found a few on the street. "Ms. Dorn," I said, "do you know how dope you are?"

Just as I predicted, when Ms. Dorn brought her passions to Mott Hall, the kids began to love her and she began to love being here. Inspiring so many scholars with her creativity and energy, she went from having one foot out the door to becoming an integral part of the team. The transformation was remarkable, but the explanation didn't involve rocket science—just human nature.

All people are better at their jobs when they are empowered within them. My role is to support my teachers—whether it's providing constructive criticism about their work, mediating between them and a child, offering professional development, making sure they have all the supplies they need, or keeping a cooler of cold water for them in the office.

And all people like what they do more if they know someone at work cares about them. I show my love for my staff by checking in with them and asking one simple question every single day: "How are you doing?"

I ended up replacing the school's original science teacher with another newbie, Ms. Bunning, who at first also struggled with discipline and creating hands on activities for the kids. A perfectionist, she had trouble hearing my feedback. Whenever I gave her constructive criticism, she showed the defensiveness that are hallmarks of a person in her twenties. "I get it," I said to her, "but I think you need to listen." And she did. The difference between Ms. Bunning and the new teachers who didn't last at Mott Hall was that she became someone willing to do whatever it took to learn.

Ms. Bunning not only learned to manage her classroom but anytime we had activities at the school, she showed up to lend her support. Soon enough she brought her own passions into Mott Hall to become assistant coach of the flag football team and run the Mott Botts, an elective she started that has become one of the school's most popular clubs. The one thing that keeps anyone grounded in this work is to connect it to personal passions—

like Ms. Achu's step team or Ms. Dorn's beekeeping—embedded within it.

Whenever outside educators visit Mott Hall, they are struck by how, after the last bell rings, teachers stay to spend time with our kids, talking to them, doing activities the children enjoy, or just sitting together. "How do you get your teachers to do that?" they always ask.

"They want to be here," I say of my team. "We all do."

CHAPTER THREE

THE SCHOLARS

Three months after Mott Hall opened, one of my mentors, Dr. Renee Young, a parent advocate and former principal, paid me a visit. She took a good long look at the data I had posted on my wall. It recorded what the scholars had achieved on their state exams the previous year, as well as results from more recent interim assessments. Then she read out five different names, turned to me, and said, "Tell me about them."

"What do you mean?" I said.

"Talk to me about these children. Beyond the numbers."

I gave her a flowery answer that combined vague generalities and education jargon.

"Nope," my mentor said. "What are their struggles? And what do they do well?"

I couldn't give her any specific answers.

"You don't know these kids," she said.

"No, I do!"

"Let me explain something to you. You work in an underserved community. And what's going to happen is everyone is going to tell you what these kids *can't* do. The data from the tests will say these kids aren't achieving. The media will say they can't act right. Your teachers will say they can't learn. It's much easier to say what kids are deficient in than to figure out what they're great at and work hard to build upon their abilities.

"So the next time I come here and ask you that question, you better have a real answer to give me," she said. "You owe that to these children."

It was a wake-up call that I was accountable to the children in my school, and one of the best pieces of advice I ever received.

My mentor's visit was right before Thanksgiving, so I took home every scholar's file and all their assessments, as well as a boxful of Post-its, and over the holiday I read every single piece of information about or by each child. The Post-its were for me to label students' strengths and weaknesses. I connected their work to their interim assessments, then looked at their grades. From examining an entire body of work, a picture emerged of a whole person, such as repeated struggles with writing or a progression in math. It was all there. (For some schools, the student population is way too big to do this for every child, but leaders can learn just as much from selecting a sample of five children at random and going through the same process.)

When I got back to school after the break, I sat with the teachers and asked them the same question my mentor had asked me. And, no surprise, they couldn't answer any better than I had. So I had them do the same activity I had just completed. I wanted to share with them the transformative experience that had sharpened my focus in running Mott Hall; if we were going to help our scholars, we needed to know them.

You can learn a lot about students and an academic environment by examining test scores, classwork, and classroom dynamics. But, of course, the very best way to get to know anyone is simply to listen.

In my earliest days of teaching, I discovered the power of listening to students. McKinney was one of the most challenging schools in Brooklyn, a huge place with about a thousand students, mostly from Fort Greene's infamous housing projects. When I arrived, I naively assumed I would be met with a roomful of kids who were ready to learn. I was not at all equipped for what I found. Those kids, who had seen and experienced a lot in their short lives, ran the school. They thought nothing of cursing out the principal, let alone their teacher. The entire school was out of control, and as a special education teacher, I had arguably the most challenging students in it.

The New York City Department of Education has protocols for how a child becomes a special education student and what that means for her or him. The process always begins with an evaluation of the child at the request of the parent or the educator. If it's the teacher who presents concerns—typically issues with reading or writing on grade level, inability to retain information, or problems getting coherent outcomes—the school is supposed to make sure that the educator has tried all the different modalities of learning and support systems available before escalating the problem. So, for example, if a child is having trouble reading, has the teacher tried using a book that is more appropriate for his or her reading level or working one on one with the student during class or after school? If the teacher and school *have* tried everything and the student still isn't learning, then an evaluation by psychologists and learning specialists is conducted to determine if a disability exists and what type of educational setting would be beneficial to the student's achievement; then this is outlined in a document called an individualized education plan (IEP).

There are three types of settings for special education. The most restrictive is the self-contained classroom for students whose learning levels are so low they need minimal distraction and maximum attention. These classes contain no more than twelve special education students, one special education teacher, and at least one paraprofessional (a teacher's aide). The next type of classroom is the integrated coteaching class, where students with special needs and those in the general population are taught together by one special ed teacher and one general ed teacher, who plan their lessons together and provide instructional support to the entire class. The last type of setting is SETSS, which stands for special education teacher support services. Here, a special education teacher provides extra support to a student in a general education classroom for anywhere from three hours a week to half of each school day, either in the classroom setting or one-on-one. The goal is always to have a student be in the least restrictive classroom possible.

The problem, especially in underserved communities like the one in which McKinney was located, is that special education becomes a dumping ground for students educators are fed up with. In particular, too many young men of color wind up in special education because of their lack of self-esteem, motivation, and self-control—none of which are ameliorated by special ed services.

That was certainly true with some of the students in my first class as a teacher, where I made so many mistakes. Faced with twenty-five children, many of whom had learning or emotional issues, I talked, talked, talked as I taught straight out of the textbook. I was so busy just trying to get through the material that I didn't stop to consider their needs. It wasn't until I started pulling aside my students and sitting with them when they had behavioral issues that I began to gain insight into who they were.

Trevor was the first boy I really talked to. He was smart but could catch an attitude. Why was he a teenage version of Jekyll and Hyde? I sat with him and asked about home. "Tell me about your mother," I said.

"My mother is dead," Trevor answered.

From there the story slowly continued. Trevor had been close to his mother, who had died from cancer. But now his dad, with whom he didn't really have a relationship, was bringing him up. With his mom gone, Trevor struggled with letting people in. He created a wall to block out his emotions because he didn't want to get attached to people, who seemed to be here one minute and then gone the next. We talked about poetry, which he loved. That's how I was able to connect to Trevor, through writing and reading poetry that spoke to his experience.

Chloe was the best-dressed girl in school, but she couldn't keep up academically. Whenever I saw her in class in the latest designer clothing, struggling to read, I wondered why the monetary investment wasn't going into helping her in school. After I talked to her, I learned she had several sisters and brothers at the school, and by the accounts of my colleagues, each had his or her own set of learning disabilities. It made me think about the mom's priorities and whether or not she struggled—she never came to school meetings, but when I saw her near the housing projects she was dressed in high-end name brands.

Once I started to get to know my students, I went beyond sitting with them after class or at lunch. Sometimes I would show up at their homes, like I did with Dion, also from my first year at McKinney. He was a little man, mostly unassuming, but every now and then a quiet rage came on and you could tell he had the capability of hurting someone. After a class where he almost made me snap with his disrespectful attitude, I said, "Oh, you must have me confused. Let's see what happens when I show up at your house."

He gave me a look like "Whatever."

At the end of the day, though, I went to the main office at school, found Dion's address, drove to his house, and waited until he came home. When he pulled up to his house and saw me there, the look on his face said it all; he couldn't believe I'd actually showed up. "I wasn't playing with you," I said. "I'm from Brooklyn and not afraid to go anywhere."

We went up to his apartment, where I met his mom and could tell instantly she had her own challenges. Whether they stemmed from drugs or alcohol, I didn't know. Still, I had the conversation I came there to have—saying that her son was out of control and I wasn't going to put up with it.

Mom said she was sorry, but her apology wasn't the

point. The point was that my showing up at his house proved to Dion that I cared (and maybe that I was also a little crazy). I never had a problem with him after that. *Ever.*

The single most effective strategy I employed in changing their behavior and improving learning outcomes was talking to the kids. I always kept it simple, starting out conversations with questions like "What did you eat for breakfast?" If they said "Nothing," I'd ask why without judgment, which led to more answers and more questions, all of which offered details about their home lives and larger circumstances they would never have offered up without being prompted.

—Who lives at home with you?
—What did you do this weekend?
—What do you *like* to do on weekends?
—Where do you go after school?

Simple, basic questions about my students' lives as they were and as they wished them to be opened up whole worlds of information one could never get from any kind of test or evaluation and helped me target how I dealt with each student. Talking with students also helped with my patience and compassion in the classroom when I knew the struggles my students were going through outside of it.

I had conversations all the time—at lunchtime, when

many kids would come upstairs to my room; after school; or on Saturdays, when I came in to tutor those who needed extra help. Once I knew about my students and they understood that I was interested in them, management stopped being an issue. I didn't worry about what was happening in the rest of the school because I knew I could control my room. The room with the most behaviorally and academically challenged students had become one filled with productive, focused individuals.

(My experience as a special education teacher is in part why, as a principal, I loathe when teachers are quick to say that a child should be put into special ed. I make sure that in my school special education is *not* a dumping ground. At Mott Hall, if a teacher brings up concerns about a child's learning ability or emotional issues, I need evidence before I will even begin the formal referral process. That means observations conducted by my own special education teachers, and anecdotes from the general education teachers on how they supported the child in class and what conversations they held with parents. If a kid is not learning in a classroom, we can have him evaluated, do all that, and then we're going to get a piece of paper that will confirm—he isn't learning. Simply put, an IEP doesn't change a teacher's responsibilities.)

It's crucial for all people who work in education, no matter what part of the country they are in, to know the needs of the children they serve beyond academics. These needs will change depending on the socioeconomic status and cultural backgrounds of the students, but wherever kids come from, they all have that basic need to be heard. This lesson was reinforced for me when in 2007 I taught high school biology to a diverse group of students in Kennesaw, Georgia. I had a real mixture of white, Asian, black, and Hispanic kids, some of whom were from trailer homes while others lived in million-dollar mansions.

The way the school day in Kennesaw was structured— back-to-back ninety-minute periods for classes with only one thirty-minute break for lunch—and the fact that most of the students were bused to and from school meant that there was no time for personal interactions. It was a major culture shock for me coming from Brooklyn, where I was used to plenty of opportunities to interact with my students. In Georgia, I asked, "When do you kids get to talk to anybody?" The answer was: never.

I thought that was insane. Even though the students were in high school, they still needed to know there were adults actively listening and readily available to talk about concerns or answer questions. So one day I announced to a biology class that I really loved, "Okay, you all. We have a different assignment to do today.

"You are going to write a letter to one person. It can be someone who you needed to say something to and haven't; or someone who left—whether it's because they walked out or they were thrown out; or someone who's died.

Whatever you did not tell them, whatever you needed to tell them—you have to write it."

They dove right into the assignment because I had connected with these kids, and when children trust you, they don't question why you are deviating from the normal script. Plus no one had ever asked them anything about themselves. The letters many of them wrote were so earnest, they made me cry. One girl used to sit up and watch TV with her grandmother (a lady she described as having a head of white hair and always a mint in her pocket). After her grandmother died, she felt a tremendous void in her life. The letter that truly broke my heart was Sheryl's. She wrote her mom to say she was angry with her for not fighting hard enough to stay off heroin, overdosing, and dying. Now she was forced to live with her dad and new stepmom, who didn't like her. To numb the pain, Sheryl, who was only in ninth grade, had entered into a sexual relationship with a senior from another school. He was her fifth boyfriend, but the attention she sought from him couldn't fill the void of the love lost from her parents.

The stories, one after the other of hidden pain and anger, were so beautiful and important I turned them into a book that I had printed up. Just as with Dion, who saw that I cared because I took that little bit of time to show up at his house, my students in Georgia understood from my printing up and binding their stories that I was invested in them. I was there not just to grade their tests but to see to their growth as people. In that way, although the colors of their skin might have been different and they lived almost a thousand miles apart, they were no different from my kids in Brooklyn.

Of course the social and emotional needs of children in underserved areas are greater, as my mentor explained, and so have a greater effect on their behavior and ability to learn. After I returned from Georgia and was accepted into the New Leaders program, I spent my residency at a Brooklyn charter school that was great at raising academic proficiency in underserved populations. It excelled in the important task of getting its students to test well and read on grade level, but it seemed to accomplish those outcomes in part by regularly punishing certain students more than I thought was appropriate. Specifically with young men, hyperactivity was misunderstood as defiance.

I started noticing it when, every day around 10:00 A.M., a few children were brought to the academic office where I worked for a "time-out." One week a nine-year-old boy named Jacob got two time-outs. Each time, he was paraded through the hallways, where teachers would ask, "What's wrong? Why aren't you in class?" The academic director, escorting the little boy, answered, "Jacob doesn't know how to sit well" or "Jacob isn't listening today."

I wondered what constituted behavior severe enough that it warranted so much lost instructional time and in such a noticeable way. I'm not against removing children from classrooms, particularly when they become a distraction to others, but Jacob's punishments made me curious. When kids are repeatedly sent out of class because they are in trouble, I want to know the root causes of their behavior. I decided to investigate while Jacob sat alone at a desk.

"So what you got going on this weekend?" I asked.

"I'm going to see my dad."

"Yeah? Where's your dad at?"

"Not sure. We take this bus ride. It's a lot of hours."

"Huh . . . Do you get to see your dad often?"

"Not really. I haven't seen him since September."

This was February. But I already knew from his mention of the long bus ride that Jacob was going to see his dad in prison.

"Wow," I said. "How do you feel about seeing him?"

"I'm a little nervous."

You didn't need a degree in psychology to know that Jacob was acting up because he didn't know how to contain himself in anticipation of seeing his father. Not to mention the stress his household was under with his mom raising him alone and doing those treks upstate. We talked a little more, and Jacob described to me how he got excited about seeing his dad but then was sad when he had to leave. I said, "You know what? Why don't we create a book for your dad?"

"A book?"

"Yeah. Tell me: who's your favorite superhero?"

"Batman."

"Okay. So why don't we make it a book where your dad is Batman and you're Robin? Because Batman can't function without Robin. It'll have a story and pictures of you. This way, when you leave, your dad will have a reminder of you. And if he feels sad like you feel sad, he can refer back to this book. I promise it'll make you feel good too, because when you start to feel sad, you'll know that he has something of you with him."

Jacob liked the idea. I took a picture of him on my phone, sent it to my e-mail, and printed it out. Then I got construction paper and a hole puncher. Jacob's face lit up. "We're going to do this for my dad?" he asked.

"Yeah."

And what was a really big deal for Jacob was *so* simple. The book that Jacob took with pride back to class was construction paper, a picture of him, a story, and some pictures of Batman and Robin I found on the Internet and printed out. It was also something he could give his dad with pride.

I felt really good about what had happened, so I was totally surprised when Jacob's teacher later sought me out to say I had overstepped my bounds. According to her, he was removed from the class for a reason and shouldn't have been rewarded by making a book. I got it. He was removed because he was misbehaving, but that didn't exclude the fact that as his educators we needed to understand *why* he was misbehaving. In this case Jacob's acting out was a direct result of not knowing how to express himself. Whose fault was that? Who do we blame for that?

I was so angry that the teacher was more concerned about territorial overstepping than about Jacob's welfare that I had to give myself a time-out at the McDonald's around the corner to calm down. I have no idea what it's like to visit your dad in prison at the age of nine, or miss your father because of some mistake he made. But I do know Jacob, and many others just like him, could easily wind up incarcerated in part from constantly being reminded that they are not good enough.

That was the inspiration behind Mott Hall: to help children like Jacob find their self-worth. And not because it's the right thing to do (which it is) or will make their dreams come true (there are no fairy tales in Brownsville). For kids who face what my scholars do every day, developing inner resources and the resilience to keep striving despite what everything else around them indicates is the *only* chance they have at something beyond survival.

Yet it is precisely the hardened traits they develop in order to survive in their neighborhood that make supporting children in underserved communities so difficult for educators. No matter how disrespectful and defiant my scholars started out as at Mott Hall, I was determined never to forget their humanity.

The fall of 2011, Mott Hall's second year, brought a

new class of sixth graders, who were more motivated than the first. Having gained a reputation as a place with caring adults, activities, and a rigorous curriculum, the school attracted some families who liked what we were doing. This was still Brownsville, though, so even if they weren't as unruly as the first group of sixth graders, most of the new scholars arrived emotionally and academically lacking.

One of the toughest kids in that class was a boy named Vincent. He was just bad. And I mean *bad*. I gave him so many chances to do better, but he never did (or he couldn't string more than a few good days together). One day he went too far. In front of his entire class, I stood face-to-face with him and said, "Vincent, let me tell you something. Today is just not your day. You think you run stuff. And you don't."

I make it a practice not to speak to kids in open spaces. Instead, I like to talk to them privately, the way most people prefer to have difficult conversations. When I do address a scholar's behavior in public, as I did with Vincent, I explain why I am doing it. "You're not listening," I say. "So since you want to act out publicly, let's have a public conversation. And when you start to feel uncomfortable, you'll understand what I feel when I have to see your disrespectful behavior in front of everyone else." The scholars know my expectations, and this awareness changes how most of them interact with me.

Vincent, however, wasn't concerned about meeting anyone's expectations. "You're going to sit in this other room," I said, sending him to the conference room across the hall, where he could work by himself until I had time for a follow-up conversation. Vincent took the knapsack that someone had left on the chair I pointed to, moved it to the floor, sat down, and went to work.

I wasn't there for what happened next, but the bag happened to belong to Amir, a very combative child. When he returned to the conference room and saw Vincent in the seat where his bag had been, he asked, "How did my bag get on the floor?"

"I moved it," Vincent answered.

"Why you touching my bag?"

"Yo, relax. I just put it on the floor next to me."

"You don't need to be touching my bag," Amir said, now raising his voice.

"Yeah? You're going to stop yelling. That's all I know. You're going to stop yelling."

Amir left the conference room and went downstairs with Vincent in tow, even though I had told Vincent to sit tight.

"Listen," Vincent said, confronting Amir. "You need to watch how you talk to me."

"What you gonna do, punch me in my face?" Amir said.

"Listen . . ."

"Punch me in my face then."

I don't know why Amir said that, but Vincent took him up on the suggestion—and punched him so hard that he fractured the kid's jaw.

The next thing I heard was screaming. Running toward the commotion, I found Amir in Ms. Achu's arms, hysterically yelling while his mouth gushed blood. We called 911, and an ambulance took Amir to the hospital.

The following day, I logged into the Department of Education's computer system to input the incident into Vincent's disciplinary record, and that's when I read about how, before he arrived at Mott Hall, before he turned eleven, he had destroyed classrooms, kicked people, and committed other acts of violence until he was finally suspended for stabbing a paraprofessional with a pencil!

Although Vincent's record detailed his violent past and revealed that he clearly wasn't afraid of adults—I mean, he put a pencil point in someone's hand—I wasn't afraid of him. I had confronted him many times without fearing the threat of him becoming violent. His troubled history didn't make me want to give up on him either.

When Vincent came back to school, I had him come to my office for a meeting. "Listen," I told him, "I read your history. You can't do stuff like that!"

"Ms. Lopez, I was trying to calm down. Amir got me upset."

This was it—the crux of the problem. In Vincent and

Amir's community, being reactive was the only way to survive. If someone does something to disrespect you, you have to come back at that person in the moment. Otherwise you are perceived as weak and become a target. But that kind of volatile behavior, while it might keep enemies away on the street, has disastrous consequences in school and in the larger society.

"Vincent!" I said. "Whenever you assault someone, you can go to jail. Because of this you could wind up in the system, which is where they want most young men of color. Amir wasn't worth it. Your life wasn't in danger. He disrespected you; I get it. But going to jail isn't worth it."

To anyone who hasn't stepped foot in Brownsville, Vincent and Amir might have appeared as either out of control or lost causes. But once you understand them in context, you gain a newfound respect for all that they've achieved.

The same fall that Vincent and Amir arrived at Mott Hall, a man on top of a building across the street from P.S. 298 on Watkins Street, just six blocks from my school, fired off more than a dozen shots from an automatic pistol at 2:30 P.M.—just fifteen minutes after the last students were let out from the school that serves children from pre-K through eighth grade. The gunman was apparently aiming for a group of gang rivals but wound up killing a mother who was picking up her child. The woman was shot to death while shielding several children. (An eleven-year-old girl's cheek was grazed, and another mom was hit in the arm and chest, but both survived.)

Brownsville is not a neighborhood where children get to be children for very long, if at all. It's in this environment that Mott Hall's scholars grapple with the challenges faced by all kids going through the tumultuous period of growth that coincides with middle school. While my scholars have a greater age range because some of them have repeated more than one grade, the typical age range for middle school is eleven to fourteen years old. It's a period when children are becoming adolescents and figuring themselves out. Hormones rage; attitudes change. They have strong personalities even as they try to find their own voices. It's a roller coaster.

Because children this age are growing physically and their attitude is larger than life as they try on different personas, adults tend to approach them as if, cognitively, they are on our level. But they aren't. In Brownsville this phenomenon is exacerbated. Like in any underserved community, many of my scholars have to raise themselves and their younger siblings in a dangerous and difficult place.

Saddled with this huge responsibility, they are forced to become mini-adults. But at the same time, they aren't afforded any of the rewards that usually come with responsibility. They don't have freedom of choice and can't reap any benefits from their efforts. In this way they are very much children—only ones who are constantly being told what to do without much room for enjoyment.

Therefore, at Mott Hall, the way classes are run and the curricula teachers use must take into account the needs of those we are serving. Otherwise we just create institutionalized spaces that scream the message: "If you don't conform to what we do here, then you don't belong." And children, especially those from places like Brownsville, who we, as educators, say we want to help the most, wind up simply not belonging in school.

There's a theory in education known as the democratic classroom, a broad term that means a setting based on mutual respect, where students are active participants in the learning process. While I believe this type of environment is essential for all children, it's of particular importance in a place like Brownsville, where many students not only are culturally alienated from the educational system but also don't have freedom in their outside lives to express themselves and explore ideas.

I'll never forget a moment when I was still a teacher and several administrators were having an impassioned conversation with an important advocate in education. "Why is it that we get kids to college, but once they're there, they don't make it?" he asked. Various opinions and theories were offered. I, a relative newcomer to education, had no business butting into the exchange among these veterans of the field. Still, I couldn't help myself.

"Have you ever asked the students what the obstacle is?" I said.

The expert was asking an important question but not tapping the best source of information for the answer: the kids.

Society's most intractable problems can only be solved through the democratic process. But that process needs to be learned. In the democratic classroom, teachers engage students with questions as opposed to lecturing them. In turn, children get to take a more active role in the lesson by driving the conversation. Not only does this process foster cooperative learning, where students work together to accomplish shared goals, but it also offers opportunities for children to express what they are interested in learning. The whole process validates *their* thoughts and beliefs. In other words, it gives them a voice.

Voice, however, needs to be developed. When scholars enter Mott Hall, they aren't sure of what they want. The concept of opinion is a new one to them, because everything has always been imposed on them. First they need to be taught the basics of how to discern among different ideas and decide which ones appeal to them. We teach our scholars how to respectfully disagree, question information with civility, and use evidence to back up their points of view. Even if tempers flare or something inappropriate is said, we take the time to go through what was said and analyze why it was inappropriate or made a peer upset.

That process is a much more effective tool for growth and understanding than getting angry or punishing the scholar.

Mastering the basics of good discussion isn't the only way we invite scholars into the learning process at Mott Hall. We also look carefully at the materials we choose to teach and try to find ones that our kids can connect to.

During Mott Hall's first year, I had my sixth graders read *The Immortal Life of Henrietta Lacks* as part of their English language arts curriculum after the vice provost of Long Island University, Gladys Schrynemakers, brought the book to my attention. When I first opened Mott Hall, I had a partnership with LIU, and Dr. Schrynemakers, an educator with a strong passion for science, was a particular champion. She recommended the *New York Times* bestseller about an African American mother of five who died in 1951 at the age of thirty-one from cancer but whose cells lived on (without the knowledge of or consent from her or her family) as the material for many scientific discoveries, including the vaccine for polio.

As soon as I read it, I bought a copy of the book for every single sixth-grade scholar. Although the level of writing was very advanced, there were a lot of ways for them to enter into that material. I knew they'd connect to a story about how race and socioeconomics influence a person's choices—and how someone discounted by the rest of the world can still have a huge impact. Sure enough, they read the book cover to cover. Sixth-grade scholars, who came into my school with a 52 percent attendance rate, 86 percent of whom were below grade level in English language arts and math, read that book every single day and got it done. (We were all excited when we went to Barnes & Noble to meet the author, Rebecca Skloot, and had her sign our books.)

Having learned of the scholars' interest in *The Immortal Life of Henrietta Lacks,* Dr. Schrynemakers worked with my science teacher to help develop the curriculum for a course revolving around Skloot's book and provided our school with the resources for the children to do a final special PowerPoint presentation at the university.

In class, the scholars broke up into groups to analyze different aspects of the book. One group focused on the contributions Henrietta Lacks made to scientific discovery; another looked at how a multibillion-dollar industry was created from her cells even as she died in poverty; a third explored the social circumstances of the times in terms of civil rights and feminism to understand the decisions Henrietta Lacks had to make as a woman of color; and the last considered the generational impact of this story of alienation and theft. The scholars weren't intimidated by the high-level material but energized by it, because they were learning through one woman's story the history of many issues that directly affected their lives.

When they presented their work at LIU, the professors

and graduate students who listened to them were amazed at the depth of the scholars' thinking and clarity. "Who *are* these kids?" the impressed graduate students asked. I wanted to say, "They are some of the most challenging kids I've ever had in my life." But I wasn't surprised by the caliber of their presentations, because I never expected anything less from them.

Classics like *Animal Farm* and *Romeo and Juliet* have obvious merit and a place in the curriculum, but when the scholars read something where the connection to their lives is more immediate, they are more likely to have those lively and interesting conversations that make learning exciting. The curriculum I created around *The Immortal Life of Henrietta Lacks* is what I push my teachers to do—not keep kids in a vacuum but use whatever material will foster rich discussion, analytical thinking, and deeper comprehension.

Middle-school-age children have gained in their creative powers, ability to ask good questions, and willingness to take risks. They are open to so many different directions and ideas; we need to do everything we can to engage them during this precious and short time. So I don't just listen to my scholars when it comes to their personal stories, but I also ask them what they actually want to learn about. They can't choose math, science, English, or social studies; but at Mott Hall they can choose electives, which is why I built them into the curriculum.

Based on a number of factors, including interest surveys written and taken by the children, talents and personalities in the class, teaching artists I can wrangle, and the abilities of staff members, my scholars have a say in the types of activities they want to do. The options change all the time, but they have taken many electives like music production and comic book design. And that's *during* school. After school they have culinary arts, Bridges Winners (a renaming of the popular fitness TV show *The Biggest Loser,* because I don't ever want my kids to feel like losers), stepping, water robotics, Lab Rats, coding class, sewing, beekeeping, and gardening.

If my scholars express an interest in a subject, I will do whatever I can to see they get to do it. This is about more than just trying to get them to like school (although that's not a frivolous goal, since children will do better in any subject if they enjoy it). My scholars in particular need to know that there is a space for them to have a voice that has nothing to do with obligation or obedience. I want them to feel comfortable asking for things that will help them and articulating the reasons. In the effort to develop our scholars' social and emotional well-being so that they do better while they are at Mott Hall, there is also a promise that these tools will serve them throughout their lives.

Understanding and managing choice, being able to question others respectfully, voicing opinion with reason and proof—these are all things that are essential to success at any age. So are healthy relationships, which is why I add friendship to the list of life skills all scholars must learn before leaving Mott Hall.

So much time and energy in middle school goes into gossip and social acceptance that it can take away from studying and being present in classrooms. If, for instance, children make poor decisions about their friends now, the effects will be with them far into the future.

With every grade that comes into Mott Hall, I have a full-out assembly for the "friends" talk, which begins like this: "Everyone is not your friend. You have acquaintances; you have peers. But you don't necessarily have friends."

This shocks the kids, because they call everyone a friend. But I get real clear on the terminology. I teach them that real friendships are proven over time with specific criteria. A friend honors and respects you—and if he or she doesn't do that or make you a better person, you should not consider him or her a friend.

"Acquaintances are people you know from the neighborhood perhaps, or people you've seen; but you don't really know them well. And then you move up to peers, people who work with you; you know them, but they're still not friends.

"*Then* you get to friends. Friends are people that you've known for years, people that you can share your stories with, people that you can trust, people that, if something happens to you, have your back. Friends have your best interest at heart, even if it means correcting you when they see you doing something wrong."

This description of interpersonal dynamics might seem simple, but a lot of our scholars live among unhealthy relationships and adults who have hurt them. For them, learning how to handle people who don't have their best interest at heart is as important as multiplying and dividing fractions.

Every single year, they have to learn they don't have friends, they have peers. And I have to remind them of the lesson throughout the year: "Is that your friend? No; that's a peer, somebody in your space."

In Mott Hall's second year, we had a group of girls who fought all the time, and at the center of it was Melissa, who thought she was better than everyone else. She insisted that she didn't come from Brownsville, even though she lived five blocks from the school, and she claimed her father was white, even though he wasn't. "My mother makes too much money for me to even be in your same circle," Melissa would taunt the other girls, even though it was doubtful her mom was raking it in as a medical assistant. "She could buy you and your whole family."

Although she was obviously insecure, Melissa was able to divide this group of nine girls, pitting them against one another by talking behind one person's back one day and another's the next, so that almost every day I had some combination, if not all, of them in my office because of a fight.

I created an individual action plan for Melissa that started out with her not being able to say anything negative—just for one day. She was allowed to write it down, she just couldn't say it to a person. "Or if you feel like you must say something negative to somebody because they're getting on your nerves," I said, "you need to find me right away." That was Melissa. But with the rest of the girls, we sat down once a week, lunch with Ms. Lopez, and talked about some of the issues they were experiencing. As I listened to them talk about why this one was a friend and that one wasn't, I had to say it again: "That's not your friend, because that person just talked about you. I heard them in the hall."

I can be blunt in that way with my scholars, because they know that, no matter what they do—even if they have outbursts or are late to class or act defiant—I love and accept them. The only time I feel like I have to say to a child, "You don't belong here," is when he or she doesn't respect the rules and regulations to the point that the behavior creates an unsafe space for everyone else. Despite our population of extremely challenging children, that is the exception.

Mott Hall is the place our kids run to when tragedy strikes. I'm always amazed when a scholar who has just lost a parent (which happens too often) returns to school right away. Jessica, who also started Mott Hall during its second year, didn't want to go home at all when she found out her mother had passed away.

Her oldest sister, Sandra, arrived at school and told us that their mother, who had been sick in the hospital, was gone. So we knew before Jessica or her younger sister, also a student at Mott Hall. Sandra and I hugged, and then she went to go pull her little sister from class.

I had planned on getting the staff together to talk about this the next day, when Jessica and her little sister would most likely be back in school. But an hour later, Jessica was walking the halls. Confused, I approached her.

"Hey, beautiful," I said cheerfully. "What are you doing in the building?"

"I had to come back," she said. "I can't deal with my sisters and my niece. All that crying. I need to do something, focus on one thing. So I don't know. I just came into class."

I sat down, but I didn't tell her how sorry I was for her loss or anything like that. Instead I said, "What can I do?"

"What can *you* do?" she said. "I don't even know what you're talking about."

"What do you need from me?"

"I'm okay."

"You want a sandwich?"

She just shrugged her shoulders. I called over one of my

staff members passing at that moment and asked him to go to the store for a sandwich.

"You want chips?"

She gave another shrug.

"Okay. We need some chips, too."

We could have sat there all day talking about her loss, but that wasn't going to help Jessica. Or we could figure out how to support her in this moment and give her what she needed—starting with a sandwich.

At the end of the day, my team and I regrouped. We came together as a family to figure out spaces and strategies that would over time support Jessica as she went through what would undoubtedly be up and down moments.

After she lost her mom, everybody here was Jessica's mom. We know all our scholars so well, and with Jessica we knew as soon as a particular expression crossed her face that she was having a moment. "Go in my office; just sit," I said whenever I saw it. Then I would immediately find Gabrielle, one of Jessica's best friends, who had lost her mom a year earlier, and say to her, "I need you to go in and talk to Jessica." They always had space in my room to have those conversations.

If someone loses a loved one, everybody here feels it. Amazed at the outpouring of emotion for her, Jessica described a moment when one of her classmates, Claudine, first heard the news and started crying. "What is she crying for?" Jessica wondered and went over to Claudine, who just said, "I'm so sorry." Then Jessica broke down, because she realized people did actually care about her. "We never used to talk at all," Jessica said about herself and Claudine. "For her to sit there and cry? I was just like, wow."

How to take pain and turn it into something productive— that is one of the greatest lessons I can give my scholars. Whether it's the development of empathy or a new relationship, I want them to take that energy from whatever problems arise and use it to do something more than they could have ever imagined.

Eddie, who came back to school the day after *his* mom died, had been working on an antibullying program as part of an entrepreneurship elective where scholars create a product or service and then pitch it. But after his mother, Tina, passed away, we talked it over and realized there was a need for kids like him who had lost a loved one to connect and share stories. "There is a Tina's kid everywhere," I said.

"I love helping," said Eddie, an inquisitive child who was shy around people he didn't know. "But the problem is that I don't know how to help myself."

"When you help others, it actually helps you help yourself," I explained.

He gave me a look like he believed what I was saying but had no idea what I was talking about. But with a little help from me and two other scholars in the entrepreneurship class, Hector and Olivia, Eddie set about creating something that would not only honor his mother but also help other kids grieving the loss of a parent.

Tina's Kid began with a Facebook page, where Eddie connected with other people by sharing his story. He posted thoughts and feelings like these:

> Miss my mom so much I'm so thankful she taught me a lot of things like cooking and cleaning but she never taught me how to live without her
>
> I know this may sound weird but doing stuff your mom liked helps it truly feel like you're with her

Part of the promise of the project was that Eddie would speak to kids at other schools about his experience. When Eddie first came to Mott Hall, his confidence was so low he had trouble connecting with other scholars. Although he had come a long way in his time with us, the loss of his mother was definitely a setback. I felt that his speaking at other schools would give him a sense of purpose as well as the knowledge that his voice also had power outside Mott Hall, which would be important for him when he left here.

When I met with the entrepreneurship group one spring afternoon, they were gearing up for Eddie's first presentation. The meeting was extremely productive. We talked about everything from the emotional (how feelings surrounding death are constantly in flux) to the practical (using the notepad feature on a smartphone to write posts, so you can take your time and edit them before cutting and pasting them into Facebook). Our biggest objective, though, was focusing on the talk, which would be a big challenge for Eddie. Each scholar described his or her task.

"I'm in charge of processing the work on the posters," Olivia said.

"I'm helping Eddie conquer his feelings with other people," Hector said.

"Eddie, when you do your speaking engagement, do you want your team around you?" I asked.

"Yes, I'd like that," he said.

"Okay, you guys will go with him for moral support and to give him feedback."

"Sometimes you choke on your words," Hector said to Eddie with all the seriousness of a colleague working on a business plan.

"I choke when I speak too fast," Eddie said, equally earnest.

"That's why you don't speak fast," Hector said. "I'm not going to lie, you are an intelligent guy. We want to hear what you are saying."

"Excellent," I said, wrapping up the meeting. "I appreciate you all."

I do. I appreciate all my scholars. They are complicated, crazy, energetic, loving, and they need to be heard. I just needed to listen to know that.

CHAPTER FOUR

THE PARENTS

As I've said, Mott Hall is a STEAM-focused school, STEAM being an acronym for science, technology, engineering, arts, and math. Although STEAM schools have the same English language arts curriculum as other public schools, there is an added emphasis on introducing children to science and math for greater literacy in fields that are important to the economy but where our education system has lagged behind.

For me, however, the STEAM approach has a greater meaning, the heart of which is *inquiry*. Asking questions without judgment in order to truly understand whatever is being studied and come up with new solutions is not just the basis for the scientific method; it informs every aspect of what we do.

You can apply inquiry to anything. Scholars understand a book by asking a series of questions like "How did the setting affect the character's development?" or "What was the author's intent when using a particular symbol?" They learn about major movements in modern art by asking, "What are the defining characteristics of cubism or impressionism?"

Asking questions is also how we as teachers and administrators at Mott Hall understand our scholars. When we want to improve our instruction, allocate resources, and create action plans that support children in their development, we first have to ask ourselves what we need to know about the child. The whole child. We have to ask questions about a child's community, previous academic experiences, friendships, and anything else that affects this child. And there is probably no greater source of impact on a child's life than the parents. We can't understand our scholars unless we understand their parents.

When Antonne arrived at Mott Hall in sixth grade, he was *angry*. He got so angry that he would walk out of his classroom, without any regard for authority, and curse all the way down the hall: "Fuck this. I don't even want to fucking be here. Leave me alone. Don't say nothing to me." In those moments it was as if he couldn't even see people he was so enraged.

Antonne was one of a group of boys who came from the same elementary school and were all put in a self-contained class. He was like a number of the other boys in that the issues that landed him in the self-contained class were purely emotional. He got so angry he couldn't focus on his work. But being with boys he had known since elementary school, where they had been allowed to do whatever they wanted, didn't help matters. After four months of mayhem, I broke the cohort up and put them in general education with paraprofessionals. It worked for most of them; they had their moments, but their behavior was nothing compared to what it had been during those first months.

Antonne, however, was still having trouble dealing with authority and managing his temper. Whenever I sat and talked with him, I saw all the good inside of him. He was mature and reflective. He knew right from wrong. I didn't want to see him continuing to struggle, so I asked his mom to come in.

I find that when I want to engage parents (or children, for that matter), bringing them into my office helps a lot, because it's not the typical principal's office. I'm a firm believer that your space speaks about you and your expectations. I decorated mine with purple upholstered chairs that are comfortable to sit in and give more of a lounge atmosphere. I covered the walls in all types of things that represent me as a person, as opposed to an administrator. There are pictures of me from important moments in my life as well as my bachelor's degree diploma from Wagner College and master's degree diploma from Long Island

University. I also cut out articles from magazines and newspapers that contain important information and print out quotes with inspiring messages. On a large purple background, there's a Victor Hugo quote: "He who opens a school door, closes a prison." That's right above the Mott Hall Bridges scholars' pledge about respect, kindness, enthusiasm, achievement, citizenship, and hard work.

Sometimes I make parents wait in my office so they can look around and get to know the human side of me. Then, by the time I start speaking to them, they're receptive to listening.

But Antonne's mom stayed defensive. "You gonna tell me about how to raise my kid?" she said.

I corrected her immediately. "I'm not saying anything like that," I told her. "I want to tell you that I think your child has great potential, and I'm sorry the system has failed you so far."

All of a sudden the hard edge turned into tears.

"I'm always getting called in, and I can't take any more time from work; otherwise we are going to be on the street. This is the first time anyone has said to me my child has something good."

She and I had a good long sit-down, during which we talked about a lot of things, including something I hadn't thought about: Antonne's dad had been shot right in front of him on a playground the summer before he started Mott Hall. His dad had survived, but I couldn't imagine what it was like for Antonne to witness something like that. To see your own father, the person who is supposed to keep you safe, gunned down can't be anything less than traumatizing. In that moment, I realized he was dealing with so much more than just his issues in school.

With nearly 40 percent of Brownsville residents living below the poverty line (the neighborhood has the largest concentration of public housing in the city) and nearly half of those sixteen and older unemployed, I have so many parents who themselves have many needs. In the Van Dyke Houses, where there are 5,620 residents, including many of my students, the median household income is $11,220 a year, compared with the citywide average of $51,865. And that number includes income from welfare benefits and food stamps. Although these people carry such heavy burdens, no one checks in with them to see how they're doing. They're adults, so they're supposed to be okay. There are no mental health resources to provide parents with their own strategies for managing their time, their relationships, their losses.

Being a parent is stressful, period. You have to constantly balance your needs with those of your child, making ends meet while being emotionally present, being both an authority and a source of love, and on and on. But in Brownsville, it is so much more than that.

I consider it part of my job to make sure parents know they can rely on me, just like Maria's mom did. Ms. Hernandez, the first to sign her child up for my school, was that parent who always showed up if we needed her to do anything, like serve food during our multicultural day or participate in a poetry event. But her health deteriorated and she was in and out of the hospital. While she was in one of her brief periods out of the hospital, Ms. Hernandez came to see me because a boy was bothering her Maria. "I want you to know about this," she said, "because if anything happens to me, I expect you are going to take care of my baby girl." Two weeks later she was back in the hospital, where she died.

I attended her funeral with my team and broke down despite myself. It was the one time I couldn't be strong in front of my staff. Ms. Hernandez, who only wanted a safe and stimulating environment for her daughter, had placed the ultimate trust in me when she chose this school for Maria. It was a weight and a gift.

Plenty of my parents come to trust me as Ms. Hernandez did, but first I have to get past the hard edge so many of them have as a self-defense mechanism. Being hard is a way to protect oneself from constant hurt.

The other reason for that hardness my parents show their children is that they have to prepare their kids to live in a challenging place. In Brownsville, where in 2013 there were seventy-two shootings and fifteen murders, there is no room for their kids to make mistakes. In the fall of the following year, a twelve-year-old boy was hit in the leg by a stray bullet while his mother watched him get off the school bus.

When walking on the wrong side of the street in Brownsville can get you killed, parents fear for their children's lives every day—and that fear can come off as cruelty if you don't know what's at stake. The only way they know how to protect their children is to be tough with them and teach them how to become equally tough.

Tiana's mom was the epitome of Brownsville hard. I dreaded the conversation I had to have with her when I asked her to come in. A young mother, she was furious before I even had a chance to say a word. Simply being called into school—even though we told her that Tiana hadn't done anything wrong—was enough to send her over the edge. With Tiana's five-year-old sister in tow, she paced in the conference room while I finished up another meeting. "I'm hot and irritated," she said to our guidance counselor, Mr. McLeod, who was trying to calm her down. "You people are nosy." She couldn't wrap her head around the idea that we were trying to help Tiana, a good kid, because I'm sure no one had ever helped her.

When I called Mom into my office, her gaze darted every which way except at me. Tiana's sister sat on one side of her mother, swinging her little legs, while Tiana, already there when her mom came in, was on the other. She looked at her mom with pleading eyes.

"Tiana hasn't been herself, and today we had you come in because . . ." I started.

What I had to say was very ugly, and I didn't know how Mom was going to react.

"According to your daughter, there is a young man who hurt her . . . He forced himself on her."

"You serious?" The mother turned to her daughter in anger. "Really? Really?"

"Mom, we felt it was important to call you in for Tiana to let you know," I said, trying to keep the tone calm. "If something indeed happened and she was forced to do something that she didn't want to do, and we don't know what she was exposed to, you may want to take her to a doctor."

Mom stood up, seething.

"I am taking your ass to a doctor," she said to Tiana. "How are you going to tell them your business and not tell me? How you doing that? I don't need everyone knowing about me."

She yanked Tiana's little sister and ran out of my office. I tried to follow her, but when she turned around and said, "I don't want to talk to you. Don't come near me," I listened. I knew this woman had once punched a principal in the face, so I kept my distance.

Returning to my office, I collapsed in my chair, overwhelmed by a mix of doubt, guilt, duty, and uncertainty.

Our top priority is to make sure that our scholars are safe, therefore we are mandated to communicate with their parents if we deem that they are not. If we said nothing, then we would have failed in our responsibility of putting a child's safety first. On the other hand, I had no idea how Mom was going to treat her daughter when they left the school.

I wondered if we could have done something differently, although I couldn't think of what that would have been. Our scholars get all the chances they need here at Mott Hall Bridges, but this isn't real life. And their parents know that.

I understand that my scholars' parents' defiance toward me is another expression of the hardness they need to survive—just as it is with their children. It's exhausting, though, to have to battle mothers and fathers just in order to help them.

A father of one of my boys, Benjamin, refused to listen to me when I told him that his son needed to take the ADHD medication he had been prescribed. I called him on the phone and into my office so many times in an effort to reason with him: when his son was off his medication, his behavior was erratic. Despite the degrees I have on my wall and the fact that I run a school where I have closely observed his son and consulted the teachers with whom he spends all day, the father didn't respect my expertise. I warned him: here we could deal with his son, but on the street his behavior was going to get him in real trouble. And it did. After his son's arrest, Dad came to my office for me to sign some forms. I could see immediately that he was humbled, but there was no satisfaction in my being proved right. I was sad that it took the police saying there was a problem with his son for him to believe it.

Although I understand the historical and cultural influences at play, moments like that I want to shout, "What is wrong with you? I'm not here to hurt you. I'm not getting anything by doing this for you other than the satisfaction of seeing you and your children succeed."

As difficult as the children can be, sometimes it's their parents who present the real challenge.

After a girl became defiant to the point of threatening— getting close enough to me to make me feel like she *might* do something—I had to call school safety in to observe how this scholar wasn't respecting boundaries. Naturally I called her home right away, and when Mom arrived, she straight-up questioned me in front of her daughter: "Who did you have to sleep with to get this job?"

I wanted to laugh. "You think I slept with someone to be in Brownsville?" I said. "I'm not going to take offense at what you said, because it means you believe that my kids are worth enough that I'd sleep with someone for them."

I did take offense, though. Mostly at how she conducted herself with me in front of her daughter. Mom was angry at something, and it wasn't necessarily me. But why would her daughter know boundaries or afford me any respect after the way her mother talked to me?

The girl eventually transitioned out of Mott Hall, not because I removed her but because she and her mother couldn't honor the school's rules. Some people feel like if they keep attacking you, eventually you'll decide that's just how they are and you'll let their children be. But I cannot do that. I approach all parents, even those who want to intimidate me, the same way. Yes, I take safety precautions, but I won't lower my expectations for anyone, because children learn by example. And what would my scholars say if they saw me let someone push me around like that? I know exactly what they'd say: "Ms. Lopez, you don't let us do it; so why are you letting that person do it?" As I said to the girl's mom before she left Mott Hall, "You can't respect me and she can't respect me, so this isn't the space for you, because I'm never going to waver from my expectations."

All Mott Hall parents are fully aware of the fact that I have high expectations not only for their children but also for them. How they may conduct themselves in a certain way outside the school won't be tolerated in my space. Other principals have called to warn me about so many parents with a history of physical or verbal aggression, but I almost never see that side of them.

A principal had told me to be mindful of one mother in particular; he had to call school security to escort her out of the building after they had an altercation. I didn't know what to expect when we met, but I found her sweet if a little standoffish. Respect is a two-way street, and just as this mother never gave me trouble, I didn't give her trouble either. When her daughter arrived at school without a uniform (apparently they were all in the wash), I didn't send her home, call Mom, or even get upset. Instead I just handed the girl, who excelled both in the classroom and out, a new T-shirt and told her to put it on. I spend a lot of money to keep extra uniforms on hand so I don't have to argue with scholars or bother parents when they have much bigger things to worry about.

I know how to love my parents up just like I do the scholars. Unquestionably, the greatest way I can prove that I care is by listening. You never grow out of needing to be heard. When a parent comes into my office angry about something that happened at school or with my staff, I say, "I hear you're upset. I'm here to help you, and we're going to get through this."

They are surprised whenever they have a complaint that not only do I not put up a defense but I follow up on their concerns. Too often school administrators automatically become adversarial with parents as a measure of self-protection. But my feeling is we have nothing to be defensive about at Mott Hall, so I'm never afraid of having open conversations among parents, teachers, children, and staff. I always tell parents my expectation is that if they have an issue, they will come to my office or call to tell me. I'm always here (I work late every night, so after they get off work is fine), and my door is always open. And when they do have a complaint about a specific teacher or staff member, I don't insist they must be mistaken. Instead, I say, "Give me a minute, Mom, while I get someone to cover that teacher's class." By having the teacher come in for a conversation, I'm honoring the parent.

There was a mom who was upset because her daughter felt my secretary had been rude to her when she went to the office to get a new MetroCard after losing the one she'd had. My secretary apparently told her she'd have to come back another day, as if the card that she used to get around wasn't important. Sitting down with everyone together allowed for an open dialogue, where the mother expressed she was upset and my secretary apologized, although she admitted to having no recollection of the event. What Mom said that stood out for me was "My daughter felt like you didn't care."

It wasn't about the MetroCard but about the expectations I had established for Mott Hall. "Mom, I hear what you're saying," I said. "Ms. Lopez said that everybody in this building cares about these kids. I don't think you were upset about whether or not your daughter would have had to come back for her MetroCard. It was the mere fact that my secretary seemed like she didn't care."

"That's right."

"And what I'm hearing my secretary say is that she didn't even realize she spoke to her since she had a lot going on. But we'll make this right. If she doesn't get her MetroCard today, we're going to give her a letter. And if for any reason you have any other concerns, just like you called me this time, call me again. I'll be more than happy to take care of it."

"Okay. Thank you, Ms. Lopez."

She never called me to complain again.

All parents need to be honored, but none more so than those in Brownsville and other underserved communities, where for too long they've been disenfranchised from the educational system. Too often those in power talk to them as though they don't know enough to be participants. Too often the blame for children who struggle academically falls on their parents' shoulders when not only do they have larger circumstances to deal with but the system blaming them makes it even harder for them to engage with their children's education.

Blaming parents for children's failure in school is unproductive. If you come from a family with books around the house, it is likely you will read at grade level. If you engage in rich discussions and are exposed to cultural events, schoolwork will be a natural outgrowth of your experiences at home.

I came from that kind of family. Although neither of

my immigrant parents graduated from high school, the importance of education and learning was ingrained in me from an early age. My father bought me an unabridged Webster's dictionary when I started school at two and a half years old. I still have that dictionary, dated 1979 by my dad, and I used it to look up words.

My dad, a photographer, and my mother, a nurse's assistant, worked all the time—even weekends. So I, their only child, went to school at an early age and for long hours. My dad would drop me off before he started work at 7:30 (an hour and a half after my mom left), and I wouldn't get picked up until 5:30.

When it came time for me to go to elementary school, my mother researched all the options and worked to get me into P.S. 93, the best choice available. Two years before middle school, my mother knew which one she wanted me to attend (and had my elementary school principal write me a letter of recommendation). Even though my middle school was in Fort Greene, which at the height of the crack era was a hotbed of prostitution, gangs, drugs, and violence, my parents didn't worry about me, because I was one of those kids whose families protect them. We were going to be the ones who made it at any cost.

That's not the reality of the parents I have gotten to know in Brownsville. If these parents grew up in the same failing school district that their children attend, how can they be expected to have the capacity to help their kids academically? Putting the onus on parents just becomes a vicious circle. We need to acknowledge that our families struggle because they are at a disadvantage.

When I consider the community in Brownsville and all of its experiences with public education, overall I see a history of disenfranchisement. The parents I've met at Mott Hall didn't choose this for themselves, and they don't want the same thing for their children. Because of that, I feel empowered to use my own experience as an example for my scholars. It can be anything from the diplomas I keep on my office wall to how I conduct myself with friends.

So after I broke up a fight in which Angelica was cursing out one of her good friends in the hallway, I brought the girl back to my office and said, "Angelica, friends don't curse at each other. They don't disrespect each other."

"Yes, they do," she said.

"Who taught you that?"

"My mother and her best friend; they do worse than curse. They fistfight."

"I don't fistfight with my girlfriends or curse at them."

She gave me a skeptical look.

"Oh, okay. You think I'm lying?"

I picked up the phone and randomly called one of my best friends.

"Hey, Tiff," I said, putting her on speakerphone. "I

have a hypothetical question for you. If I called you the B-word, would you be okay with that?"

"So *who* were you calling today?"

"I have a scholar in my room. And we were having a conversation about friends. And she said that she's witnessed best friends fighting each other, like physical fights."

"You're my girlfriend, so I love you like you're my sister. And I will protect you like you're my sister. So the idea of physically becoming aggressive toward each other is just not acceptable. A person who is willing to hurt you like that would actually be considered an enemy."

"Thank you so much."

Angelica still didn't believe me. "That's just one of your friends," she said.

"Well, that one has known me since I was eleven, but let me call another one I've known since my midtwenties."

When I got this friend on the phone, I posed the same question to her. "I have a scholar in my room and she's under the impression that friends curse at each other."

"Where's she from?"

"Brownsville."

"Okay, well, I'm from Fort Greene projects. And I've witnessed those types of relationships. But those are really not your friends. Sometimes, because of the way we were raised, and because we're in a situation where we don't have what others seem to have, we like to hurt each other. But whether you have or not, your friend is supposed to be that person who protects and loves you. So when it comes to Ms. Lopez, she created a girls' group just for us, as friends, to be together in spaces with people who are going to honor each other."

After we hung up, I said, "I could call all of my friends. They're going to tell you the same thing. No one can curse at me. No one can physically touch me. That's not what I do."

In moments like that one with Angelica, I'm stepping in to expose scholars to ideas of relationships and ways of living that they haven't been exposed to before. Instead of continuing to blame parents who don't have the capacity, I teach their children how to manage themselves—and even how to support their parents.

I don't look down on my parents. I have real conversations with them just as I do with their children, meaning what I say isn't scripted or policy-driven. When I talk to them, it's from the heart and not to make them feel less-than.

My aim is not to change anyone but to make people aware—of what is available to them, of how they can participate in their children's education no matter their own level of education, and of what expectations they should have of the system serving their sons and daughters.

For example, we instituted a college fair at Mott Hall, because there is a lot of talk about "college and career readiness," but those aren't much more than buzzwords around here. How do we talk about college and career readiness when we have parents who have never been to college and don't understand what's involved in the process? Culturally, we have adults who want the best for their kids but don't have any strategies to get them there.

It's crucial to bring parents into the conversation, because no matter what educational system is in vogue or who the chancellor of the Department of Education is, the role of the parent never changes. Nothing—not the best principal in the world or the latest innovations in learning—can replace a present and engaged parent.

One of the issues that I face in getting parents to take a more active role in their children's learning is insecurity about their own academic abilities. I have so many parents who say, "If I don't understand the work, how can I help my child with it?" It's a problem I understand intimately, because as early as my elementary school years my mother made it very clear that I was on my own when it came to homework. "You're responsible to ask questions to do your work," she told me, "because I can't help you. I don't know this American work."

While I was in Ms. Veroni's fourth-grade science class, I returned home one day with a 30 on a test about pulleys.

"How could you get a thirty?" my mother asked. When

I told her that Ms. Veroni hadn't gone over that material, she took off from work the very next day so she could meet with my principal to find out what happened. If I had told my mother that I hadn't studied, it would have been a different story. The principal investigated and discovered that everyone in the class had failed the test. Ms. Veroni had messed up by running through pulleys once and then testing us on it the next day, which is not how students that age learn a concept. There needs to be review and practice of what has been taught for students to master the information. So we were all allowed to take the test again, and that time I got an 85, which was more in line with my mother's expectations.

I tell that story to my Mott Hall parents all the time as a way of illustrating that even if you don't understand the work, you can monitor what and how your child is doing by asking him or her, reviewing his or her homework, and talking to the teacher. I had so many parents who didn't come in to get their children's report cards that I paid for a system so they could get them online instead. And still, some of those parents don't check their children's grades. How is that possible?

"You're always supposed to be aware of what's going on," I say to my parents, which is why I communicate with them constantly—through letters, e-mails, meetings, and phone calls, many, many phone calls, all to keep them up to date on what's happening with their children. They know that if their child is late to school, they will get a phone call. If their child is fighting, a phone call. Never have their uniform? Phone call. I don't leave any room for parents to say they didn't know what was expected of them. "If you don't know what's going on, you're supposed to ask," I tell them. "Otherwise you chose not to know."

The need for parents to physically show up for their children's education is something I repeat over and over in one-on-one conversations and even on the wall of the school, where we have a sign with specific directives for parents:

—Parents, you must show up and be present.
—You must ask what your scholar learned every single day.
—You must check your scholar's backpack and notebooks every single day.
—You must have your scholar sit and read to you or with you every single day.

These are the key, basic ingredients for the parent's or caregiver's role in the academic success of children—and *anyone* can do them. I reinforce the message whenever I have the opportunity to give a speech in front of the parents, like at graduation or orientation. I always start off orientation for new parents by thanking them for choosing Mott Hall and entrusting us with their children. But then I caution them: "They're your children first. You don't ever give up what's most precious to you and let somebody else control that." Maybe some principals would see that kind of message as eroding their own power, but I can't see how real education is anything but a partnership. As I explain to my parents all the time, there are things I can do, things within my power, and other things "I need you to help me with.

"I work night and day, weekends and holidays, to make sure Mott Hall is *that* place for your kids. But you can't think that because you chose a great school, it is supposed to be the be-all end-all. My staff and I, we can't do this alone. *You* need to get the scholars to school on time. *You* need to see that they actually study. *You* need to get angry when they don't fulfill their promise. We're showing them where they need to be, so you need to show up as the parents and make sure that they get there."

If I wasn't 100 percent sure of that premise before, it was proven to me as my first couple of groups of sixth graders prepared to graduate. In the class that had started in the second year of Mott Hall, I had a difficult but talented boy, Terrance.

It was because of Terrance that I initially approached Coach Randy about helping out at Mott Hall. A Brownsville native, Coach Randy was working as a family counselor and coaching basketball at a local high school when I reached out to him. As a teenager, he had used basketball to stay out of the trouble that's so easy to find in this neighborhood. He and his friends would set up three games a day so that by the time they came home at night, it was all they could do to stand upright. That drive and focus paid off when he made it to college, no small feat coming from a place where less than 10 percent of the residents have a bachelor's degree. Even more impressive to me was the fact that Coach Randy decided to return to Brownsville after college to make a difference. In fact, he lives just up the block from the school.

Terrance, who was always on the verge of failing even though he was so smart, told me he wanted a basketball team. I said, "If that's going to keep you off the streets, I'll do it." And that was the inspiration to bring Coach Randy on board, even though he was only in his twenties when I offered him the position of Mott Hall's director of scholar affairs and head basketball coach. It's important on many levels to have residents from Brownsville in the school. He is an example to the scholars and their families that people from the community do go to college and have careers. It's a two-way street, though, as he also lends Mott Hall credibility within the community. There is more buy-in and trust when one of their own is working in the building.

Coach Randy is my boots on the ground. He knows about beefs going on in the streets that I don't, because, as much as I'm invested, I don't live in Brownsville. Because he is a true member of the neighborhood, he focuses on disciplinary issues from the vantage point of how we can better partner with parents to support our scholars. If he has to make home visits, he will. If a child or family needs the help of an organization, he'll find it.

But despite everything Coach Randy and all the adults at Mott Hall tried to do for Terrance, he wasn't able to walk at graduation. A fast talker with a captivating style, Terrance could come up with an intricate rap off the top of his head. He also had natural academic ability. Even though he had sixty absences that year and didn't do any prep for the state exams, he still passed all of them. Despite proving he had the academic ability required by the state to make it to high school, he failed as a Mott Hall scholar. He didn't meet any of the criteria to walk in our graduation, including the basics of showing up to school and doing the work for his courses. It broke my heart to see him waste his talent because he had the makings of a great lawyer. We were lucky to get him into one of the city's transfer high schools for students who have dropped out or fallen behind in credits (these are public schools that have been designed for overage and undercredited students—i.e., students who have repeated grades several times for whatever reasons—to graduate on time).

Meanwhile that same year, Vincent, the boy who'd had a restraining order put on him after he smashed his classmate's jaw, was able to walk. (Incidentally, he and Amir ended up being great friends. Looking at the two of them hanging out together at prom, you would never have imagined what had gone down three years earlier.) So what was the difference between Terrance and Vincent? Family.

Vincent had family members who pushed him. Whether it was his mom or his stepfather, someone was always there if I called home. He had people to protect him. Terrance—who had no relationship with his father and a mom with nine other children—didn't have anybody like that.

For a child to succeed, there has to be someone backing me up when I say, "You are going to make it." And it doesn't matter if that person—mom, dad, uncle, grandmother, cousin—didn't have the capacity to make it himself or herself.

Recently, I was doing some paperwork in the conference room after school had let out when one of my scholars, Benjamin, the boy with ADHD who had been arrested, walked in with his dad, who said, "I had an argument with this young man that I need you to weigh in on. I told him he needs to read more, so he can advance his level. But he says to me, 'Dad, why are you always trying to push me?' Ms. Lopez, help me out, because this is hurting my heart."

I was totally surprised—not that Benjamin was giving pushback but that his dad was asking me for help. For two years I had tried to have this conversation with him, explaining to the father how Benjamin was all over the place in school and drained a lot of energy from his teachers. Anything you asked Benjamin was met with the same answer: "No." But his dad refused to believe anything I was telling him, including how we could help Benjamin.

"I don't see that with him," he would say. "He doesn't give me that. I've taught him. He knows better."

"Well, when he comes here he doesn't show that he knows better."

I suspected that Benjamin's father resented that a woman was questioning him, because his reactions were all self-aggrandizing. I would be lying if I said it didn't make me angry when he questioned my intelligence even though I dealt with his son all day, every day. But here we were. It's not about me winning but about me making *them* win. Whether Benjamin was now demonstrating to his father what he had shown us, or his dad had started to buy into the message that we all need to have high expectations for our scholars, I was more than happy to have this conversation, again.

"Benjamin, when you leave us for high school, you're going to have to come with your own sense of discipline," I said. "Your dad won't be there. Ms. Lopez won't be there. In high school, if you're failing, no one is going to call your father, because a certain level of maturity is assumed. They'll let you fail. They will let you be an eighteen-year-old sitting in a freshman homeroom class. They're okay with that. You can't do that. You've come so far.

"Remember the other day, when I went into your math class and moved your seat, because as long as you can stare out the window, you're not going to concentrate on the board like you need to? That's me knowing you, and knowing what you need. In high school, you're going to have to know for yourself that you can't focus and ask the teacher if you can move your seat. Does that make sense?"

Benjamin, a small, slim kid who usually wore a knowing expression, looked down at the floor in silence.

"I need words," I said. "Yes?"

Still nothing, so I launched into my talk on legacy, another theme I do my best to drill into my scholars' heads.

"You know, legacy is about leaving something behind. It can be an idea or a real thing. You can leave it for your kids or for anyone who comes behind you. It should be an example of something that's great. You're leaving a legacy at Mott Hall. Kids who come behind you are going to look to you and all that you accomplish, like going to college, to know what they can do. So there's no excuse for you not to succeed. At the same time, you, Benjamin, are your dad's legacy. Everything he's instilling in you is part of his legacy. You have to understand the power of that . . ."

And then Dad said, "I need to add to that. When Ms. Lopez says legacy, she means that you are more than I am.

You've seen me make a lot of mistakes, and I've done a lot of wrong. I still do wrong. But I can't have you making those same mistakes."

That was powerful. By admitting where he had fallen short as a father, Benjamin's father had more of an impact on his son than I ever could. On the streets of Brownsville, any sign of weakness is dangerous to the point of a death wish. But in that moment in Mott Hall's conference room, there was great strength in vulnerability. Instead of projecting his own inadequacies and disappointment onto his son, Benjamin's father was able to own them so that his son could have permission to do better.

CHAPTER FIVE

CONNECTED TO SUCCEED

Ever since I opened Mott Hall, I've hated summertime. Well, *hate* is too strong a word. But summer is not an easy time, because I worry about my kids out on the streets or holed up in apartments with nothing to do and no one to look after them. I watch the news every morning, hoping that I don't hear the word *Brownsville* or see one of my scholars' faces.

The summer of 2013 was a particularly bad one for young men of color. The killing of Trayvon Martin in Florida the year before had served to highlight what everyone at Mott Hall already knew: black youths were in constant peril. So did the release earlier that summer of *Fruitvale Station,* a film about the last day in the life of Oscar Grant III, a twenty-two-year-old unarmed African

American who was shot in the back by a white transit officer on a subway platform in Oakland, California.

That summer also marked Mott Hall's third year, when we reached the full scope of my original proposal. From 45 sixth graders and 5 teachers, we had grown to 15 teachers and 194 scholars through sixth, seventh, and eighth grades. I had finally been able to hire a guidance counselor, Mr. McLeod, who became an integral part of the team almost immediately. He had a lot of great ideas and such positive energy. His inspiration was the high school he had worked at before coming to Mott Hall, a place where students *did not* succeed. "I've seen what happens to kids who don't make it into good high schools, the impact that has on the trajectory of their whole lives," he said at his interview. "That's why I want to work in a middle school and make a difference."

At Mott Hall we begin our extensive high school selection process in sixth grade. There are an intimidating number of high school choices in New York City—upward of five hundred—so we start by surveying the scholars' interests to narrow them down. In the sixth and seventh grades, our students actually start visiting high schools to see how the real thing compares to a description in a book or online. On top of all the ordinary aspects students and their families look for (good teachers, courses that will prepare them for college, sports and other activities they want to pursue), we have a whole other set of concerns for our scholars—particularly our boys.

Transportation to and from the school is always an issue. Because of gang violence in Brownsville, we have to be strategic about where we send our scholars. We've seen high schools that are really good in Williamsburg (another Brooklyn neighborhood), but to get there from Brownsville, you have to take the L train, and that means going through the Seth Low housing project, and a scholar might not be able to do that without running into gang territory. So that scholar can't go to that school, and it's incumbent on us to find a comparable school on the 3 train, which he can navigate easily. Even if we feel there are schools that are better matches, we have to think about our scholars' safety first.

Mr. McLeod goes way beyond helping our scholars find the right high schools. He does guidance seminars with the students on how to conduct themselves on social media and how to understand their digital footprint. He's constantly having conversations with them about why their grades and being responsible in the classroom matter. This isn't just with kids who are having trouble; he checks in with everyone. He probably has the numbers of every single parent at our school in his phone. Because he truly wants to see the kids succeed and to be a constant part of their progress, he comes into school on Saturdays and in the summertime.

And that's where he was one late summer morning in 2013, not long before the start of Mott Hall's fourth year. I admitted to him and a few other staff members who were there, including Coach Randy and Ms. Achu, that I was emotionally spent from the recent news that a sixteen-month-old had just been killed in Brownsville. The gunman was aiming at a rival gang member, a dad pushing a stroller, and he missed.

When so much signaled that the lives of our scholars didn't matter, how could we make them believe otherwise?

From day one of Mott Hall, I had made it my mission to teach kids they mattered. That goal informed so many of my decisions, including who I hired as staff. I made sure I had male teachers of color, not the norm in New York City, because I needed men in the building who could talk to my boys. And despite the powerful role models Mr. McLeod and Mr. Millard presented, it was still important to bring in other voices, because kids aren't stupid. They know teachers are paid to be at school, so sometimes they are like, "Yeah. I hear you saying it, but you're *supposed* to say that to me," as opposed to, "Wow, this person actually took time out of his day to come talk to me."

So during Mott Hall's first year, we started a program called My Brother's Keeper, in which I brought in adults from outside the school—fashion designers, music producers, mental health personnel, and college students. These men, who donated their time and expertise (no one who participates in these types of programs gets paid), rotated through classes to talk to the boys for a half hour. The point was to get the scholars in tune with individuals they wouldn't normally have access to. I even got General Steele, a well-known rapper from Brownsville, to show up.

I went into My Brother's Keeper confident of my ability to reach out to the community because of my past success with organizing workshops for young people, which began when the principals of Urban Assembly Institute (the girls' school I worked at) asked me to create an event in honor of Black History Month. I decided I was going to do a really big event, mainly because I don't do anything small.

For a panel discussion I found fourteen high-powered, interesting women—including one who served as New York State comptroller and Tracie Strahan from Channel 4 News. They would provide a positive representation of black history through a female lens. Because I wanted this to be a real, important, multilayered experience for the girls, I approached UAI's partner school, Polytechnic Institute of New York University, to see if they could give me the space for the program. This way, not only would the girls get to hear these wonderful women but they would also have the benefit of exposure to a college atmosphere. I was thrilled when Polytech offered a room near the president's office and set about having programs printed up, but only ten days before the event, the college canceled on me. Maybe someone decided that having 160 middle school kids show up wasn't such a great idea.

In my scramble to find another location, I called my former professor Colleen Walsh at Long Island University. "Colleen, I need space," I said, not knowing if it was even possible for her to help me at this late date. She put me in contact with the head of community outreach for LIU's School of Education, who in turn put me in touch with the school's dean, Dr. Evelyn Castro. "We would be honored," she said.

The way it turned out, everyone was honored to be a part of the experience of educating and inspiring these 160 girls. The fourteen women, all of whom showed up, spoke about how beautiful it was bringing everyone together. Even Dr. Castro, who attended, was amazed. "How did you do this?" she asked.

"All I did was ask people to show up," I said. "And all of these women said yes."

"Anytime you want to do something, call on us and we'll give you the space," she told me.

I took Dr. Castro up on her offer, and building on the momentum of the Black History program, I did another event, opened it to other schools, and three hundred girls showed up. I wound up doing four events at LIU that year, including two just for boys, because they needed something like this just as much. Even though I was working at an all-girls school, it was no problem finding students to attend, because principals from other schools were excited by the symposiums—and the fact that they were free—so they sent their kids.

I loved the community events just as much as everyone else did, because they made me feel like I was really doing something good. I also always believed my work shouldn't be contained in one building or affect only one group of children. When I was organizing the programs, most people who participated or attended had no idea that I worked for the Department of Education. They thought *this* was my job.

It wasn't a job in the sense of making money, however. Thanks to LIU, I never had to pay for the space, and I never paid any of the speakers. As I told Dr. Castro after the first event, it was always about the power of asking. Basically, if you ask, most people will say yes. Of course, they can say no. (The people who said no underestimated the vision.) Even if some do say no, someone else is going to say yes. For every no, there's going to be a yes.

Many adults were fearful to talk in front of a group of kids, but by the time the event ended, they all said, "Nadia, when are you doing another one?" The thrill wasn't just about discovering the power they had in them to inspire others but also about experiencing how good it felt for someone just to listen. There was a true give-and-take, and many long-lasting connections were formed.

From asking so many different kinds of people to participate in these events, I started to develop a wide network of contacts that I maintain to this day. I gained a reputation—someone described me this way: "She is a beast." Everybody knew that. *Everybody.* When one man didn't show up to a panel, I found his friend and said, "When you see your boy, just let him know I was waiting. And it's okay that he didn't make it, because I had backups. But you don't do that to children." Some underestimated or didn't understand the magnitude and professionalism of what we were doing, but people quickly learned that if I asked, they should show up.

And I was shameless when it came to approaching people, free from self-consciousness because I wasn't asking for me; I was asking for kids.

During the time I was organizing one of my all-male summits, I was driving in Brooklyn when I spotted a man putting up signs advertising for odd jobs. I pulled over and said, "Excuse me, what do you do?" He looked startled, and I realized I had to dial it back.

"I'm sorry. Let me start over. My name is Nadia Lopez," I said and handed him a card. I was so enthusiastic about my youth summits that I had made up cards with talking points for when I approached people like this man. "I'm a teacher. I also do community events. And I didn't mean to run up on you. But I wanted to know why you're putting up the signs."

"I have my own business. I do furniture cleaning, stripping of floors, and stuff like that."

"How did you start doing that?"

"Well, you know."

"You've done time?"

"I did. I did some time."

"Okay. Well, I don't need to know the history behind it. So why are you doing this now?"

"Because I can't find a job. And I wanted to do something."

"And so you're perfect. I need you to be at LIU for an event I'm doing for boys. I need your information."

He said all right and gave me his information. After I e-mailed him and then called him, he agreed to come, and he turned out to be one of the best panelists I ever had.

"When you boys have your pants sagging," he said to the audience, "I need you to understand what that means in jail: you're giving up your goods to another dude."

The expressions on the boys' faces were shock. They were like, *"What?"*

"Yeah. When I look at y'all with your pants sagging, I'm like, huh. Do that in jail and see how far you get without getting raped."

Standing in the back, where the boys couldn't see me, so that I, the only woman in the room, didn't make them feel uncomfortable, I took in the important moment. This was what I wanted to see—a community of men having raw conversations. See, men never talk to boys, because there is an unwritten rule they should learn on their own. There is a prevailing mentality that boys have to go through the worst in order to learn to "be a man." But I question that premise. "Why?" I would ask the men who put it forth directly. "These are children. They're not supposed to know. Don't you wish someone had talked to you when you were their age?"

But during this afternoon spent at LIU, men were having discussions with boys about family issues, relationships, education, and work. In a community where there is such a sense of emptiness, the men were pouring experience, guidance, hope—really themselves—into the younger ones, saying, "You are not alone."

I continued to organize the youth empowerment summits even after I left UAI, because they were so meaningful, impactful, and successful. I knew therefore that when I opened Mott Hall, they would be part of the fabric of the school.

So I was totally caught off guard when My Brother's Keeper didn't work at my school. That first year was so tumultuous that I wasn't able to plan a special event outside school hours, but when in Mott Hall's second year, I hosted a weekend symposium, only about thirty-five people showed up—and that included the adult panelists. Based on my earlier experience, I had thought I would get at least a hundred. I decided it was an anomaly. They can't all be great events, right? But the next year, it was the same thing. Maybe seventy people attended our Saturday event. *Where are the men?* I wondered. *Where are the boys?*

I was bewildered, because I couldn't think of a place where boys and men needed to connect more than in Brownsville. Terrance—my scholar who hadn't walked in his graduation because he basically stopped coming to school—came to mind. I had tried to connect him with men while he was at Mott Hall. When the head of a local community organization came to school, he and Terrance had hit it off and he gave Terrance a pile of books, which excited Terrance and made him feel special. But the community organizer, who moved away after he got another job, never returned to Mott Hall. While the loss was hard for me, it was par for the course for Terrance. Kids like him are used to having men disappear. The result, though, is that Terrance and others like him learn to identify with the neighborhood guys who are always waiting outside.

I had worried about my boys from the day I started Mott Hall. But the troubling events happening to young men of color across the country and right around the corner made that concern first and foremost on my mind as Mr. McLeod and the rest of us tried to have a planning meeting for the 2013–14 school year. Unable to concentrate on schedules or classroom assignments, my mind kept wandering back to the same question: how do they know they matter?

Then it hit me. It was the same as everything else at Mott Hall; we just had to keep telling them over and over in different ways, including the name we gave the support group we created for our boys.

"I'm changing My Brother's Keeper," I declared, "to I Matter."

It might not have seemed like a big change (especially to my staff members, who were eager to move on to the million other things on our to-do list). But altering the name of this action group completely changed people's perception of the group and their willingness to participate in its events.

My Brother's Keeper implied the idea of men taking care of other men. That seemed to mean asking the men I wanted to reach to do something they had never been taught to do. There was no way they were going to put themselves out there like that. Meanwhile, the message of I Matter was "I am important enough to receive something I need and want." Instead of being in charge of other people, this was about affirming yourself.

When we held the first of our four annual I Matter empowerment summits for eighth-grade boys, which we opened up to the larger community, the response was immediate. We got the word out through flyers and social media. We also sent e-mails to a long contact list, which included administrators at other schools, community leaders, and individuals who had attended events I had held in the past. At least two hundred boys and men attended the summit about government and the criminal justice system. That was all it took—a name change!

We chose this theme because the law and law enforcement were pressing issues for my boys. We held the event at Brooklyn Borough Hall, a first for the building that houses the Brooklyn borough president. I leveraged my relationships to find individuals who would fit the theme. All the guests were either people I knew or others who came recommended through people I knew. On that panel were five people representing community engagement, civil service, politicians, and police officers. And the panelists weren't just any members of those professions but top in their fields, like Eric Adams, a Brownsville native who was then a state senator. It was predicted at that event that he would be the next borough president. However, he posed a challenge to the boys: he needed them to do their job as scholars so he could do his. The following January he became the first African American to hold the position of Brooklyn borough president.

This was an important event for our boys. They don't respect law enforcement personnel and don't understand government officials because no one has ever spoken to them about what these people do. No one has ever told them their rights or how to conduct themselves, explained to them the implications of their behaviors and why people see them in a certain way. No one has ever explained what these boys are truly up against every single day.

After that summit, we hosted a second one, about health and wellness, at Brookdale Hospital. Here it was the location of the event that was crucial in shifting perspectives. Brookdale is notorious in Brownsville as the "murder hospital," because the media has associated it with a place where people go to die from gunshot wounds. "The shooting victim was taken to Brookdale" is all these boys hear of the medical center.

In approaching Khari Edwards, Brookdale's vice president of external affairs, I was very specific that for my panel I didn't want doctors or the nurses whom the kids see all the time. I wanted anybody else instrumental in keeping the hospital running. This was a great opportunity to have these young men reengage with civic institutions that should be places of safety but instead have come to represent another threat. It would also introduce them to careers they had never heard of before. And so we had eight terrific panelists, including the engineer in charge of ventilation at Brookdale (no one ever thinks that the ventilation in a hospital works because someone is in charge of it) and the head of the cafeteria. The cafeteria! After the hospital made food for the kids, they saw Brookdale in a totally different light.

These summits were powerful and life changing, but

the original goal was to get as many boys as possible to attend. So I asked myself, *What will bring the most kids out on a Saturday?* The answer was pretty obvious: sports. So our third summit, Behind the Athlete, was an important milestone, but it was a true test for how much impact we could have on the community.

We had nearly three hundred people show up, lured by the reputation we were building with our youth summits as well as the topic. On the panel, in addition to a sports agent and a lawyer, there was a man who had been a phenomenal high school and college basketball player but had never made it beyond that onto a professional team. He told a story very different from the fairy tale of sports lifting the athlete out of poverty and obscurity. "I thought I was better than what I was," he said. "I went down the wrong path, ended up getting incarcerated, and didn't even finish college."

The idea that everyone, even great basketball players, struggles was crucial for these boys to hear. But the surprise, at least for me, was the effect the summit had on the men who had accompanied the boys to the event. In particular they were energized by the lawyer, who specializes in helping organizations purchase and rebrand teams. At the end of the event, the men moved the kids out of the way because *they* wanted to speak to the panelists. "Who can I talk to? I've had ideas." I could tell that no one had taken the time to invest in these fathers, uncles, cousins, and other men—and they, too, were thirsting for this kind of information and guidance.

The last summit we hosted that year addressed financial literacy and entrepreneurship. The aim was to present people who had created their own financial and business opportunities. The reality for boys like the ones who attend Mott Hall is that, because most channels of success are closed off to them for socioeconomic reasons, they will have to work that much harder to create their own paths.

On this panel were young men who didn't have a boss they needed to ask permission from in order to pursue their ambitions. There was Steven St. Fleur, who, as a seventeen-year-old working at Dr. Jay's, a chain of famous sneaker shops in New York, had recognized that certain sneakers would become hot commodities when they were "vintage." He invested in his idea by buying up those sneakers using his employee discount, and holding them. A year later, when they became collectibles, he put them online and made so much money that he quit Dr. Jay's and started his own company that eventually managed e-commerce for Russell Simmons's empire.

"I was born and raised in Flatbush, and my parents are from Haiti," he told our audience. "They didn't have the means, so I created my own means. By the time I was eighteen years old, I took care of myself. So there is no excuse," he said.

The kids could see: "This guy is no different than we are." There was a lot of hope in that for boys who don't have many images of hope around them. But whether it was the sneaker exec or the professional DJ also on the panel, the importance of education was always a focus. "I go around internationally spinning records, and I get paid for it," the DJ said. "But understand, I have two degrees. So don't get it confused."

You don't need to be an expert in education or child psychology to know that having an international DJ tell kids that they need to stay in school is way more compelling than having them hear it from their principal.

Widening prospects, presenting positive role models, and encouraging truthful and important communication between generations—these were all the goals of Mott Hall's youth summits. But because the events weren't just for Mott Hall scholars, there was another, equally important by-product: connecting young men who under typical circumstances couldn't interact with one another without violent repercussions because of gang affiliations.

We always hold our I Matter events off campus, at a college, organization, or institution such as Brookdale Hospital, so that the boys can all be in the same space. In their regular lives, they can't be seen talking to one another without inciting some kind of turf war. But while they're in our spaces, they will engage constructively. Even though all bets are off when they are back out on the street, there have never been any problems during our summits.

That's not to say we haven't had some challenges. Boys will be boys. At one event, after somebody said, "Please give a standing ovation for Principal Lopez," a group of boys decided that they weren't going to stand. It wasn't anything personal, or even a reflection on the event. It was simply a reflexive act of defiance, a holdover from the outside world, where to submit to another's request is a sign of potentially fatal weakness. I got it, but if these boys were going to grow into men who could succeed in places beyond Brownsville, they had to learn the difference between spaces like this and the street.

"You know," I said, "it's okay if you don't want to stand, because I'm not here for that. But when someone who cares about you tells you to do something, and it's a man of color who's telling you, you might want to think about doing it. Because if you're outside, in the street, and you're pulled over, and you're told to stand, to kneel, to sit, you're going to be forced to do it. And if you don't do it, it will be your life.

"Bringing you all into a space with important people who are doing this for free means that I know how to leverage my relationships. There may be something down the line that you need or want, but I'm going to remember your faces. And I might not be so inclined to give you a chance because of what you exhibited today.

"I'm not saying this to be mean or spiteful. I love you enough to have this summit, because this isn't part of my job. See, I want you to learn this lesson: people are always watching you, even making assumptions when you don't realize it."

The boys got up, and at the end of the summit, they told me they were sorry. They just needed to be reminded. Everyone needs reminders, and I consider it one of my biggest assets that I never tire of reminding. My girls are no different than my boys in that they need positive role models and stories to learn from. Their issues, however, are completely separate. If the overarching thrust of I Matter is to get men and boys to talk to one another, She Is Me, the corollary to I Matter, is a celebration of women.

The main trait I observed in my girls was the destructive anger they felt toward one another. From scholars like Angelica, who thought fighting with friends was okay because she watched her mother do it, I recognized that as women we don't necessarily know how to have healthy relationships. We need to stop fighting and start honoring one another. But that takes trust, and I understood intimately my girls' problem with developing that quality. My conflict around trust began when my dad left and I had to keep it a secret. I always walked a fine line between trusting people enough to be protected but not enough to reveal private details about myself. I was just lucky to find a circle of friends who could accept my shortcomings, because in order to get as far as I've gotten, I had to have these great relationships—people who I can call and say "I need a hug," and who will drive from Westchester to Brooklyn to give me just that.

A big problem I noticed for my female scholars was that they used their perceived differences to judge—and ridicule—one another, instead of understanding that their similarities were way greater than their differences. Girls might come from different households, but they could acknowledge, "I had a struggle and you had a struggle; both of us had something that caused us to lose our innocence as children."

At the core of She Is Me is a celebration of commonality. Maybe you struggle with math while I'm good at it, or you live with your grandmother while I have two parents, but we're all in the same boat. Just as with I Matter, in She Is Me, the adults were as integral to the events as the scholars, because as women we need to tell our girls that we've gone through periods when we didn't feel good enough about ourselves, but no matter how bad it got, there was something that pulled us through. I wanted the women in this community to have the opportunity to be the people who pull someone else through.

She Is Me was successful from the very first summit, because anytime you invite women to come together and it's free, they'll come. We didn't have a problem getting a hundred women the first time, then two hundred women, then three hundred, and so on. The conversations, which included topics such as maintaining standards and self-esteem in this age of social media, were so effective and needed that She Is Me spawned a program at Mott Hall during school hours for at-risk girls. Although we put signs up for the new club throughout the school so girls could self-select to join, there were also some whom we strongly urged to attend (in other words, we said, "Be there").

Jessica, the girl who came right back to school after learning that her mother had died, was part of that first group to join She Is Me as an eighth grader. So was Sabella, another eighth grader who was confident enough in herself to dream of becoming a plus-size model. But her bravado often veered into anger; she was the type to make fun of herself first, before anyone else got the chance. Once a week I met with these girls, who fit the mold that typically slips through the cracks. No one says anything bad about them, but no one says anything good either. Because they're not an issue, we don't pay attention to them and they quietly fail.

The She Is Me group had the hard conversations, but we also had fun. One of my favorite sessions was when we brought somebody in to teach the girls about etiquette by having a tea party. They put on pearls and hats while learning how to sit; chat; use the right fork, knife, and spoon; and drink tea. It didn't require a lot of money or planning (basically a trip to the dollar store and the supermarket) to feel fancy for a moment.

Feeling fancy, special, important, all of it—that is the

point. Kristin Suggs, a model who founded a confidence-building organization called 2Dare2Be, threw herself into that mission after she came to one of our meetings to speak to the girls. She brought along not only a few of her model friends to talk about their journey in the industry, but also T-shirts and food, so that it felt like a real event. The meeting inspired Kristin to host a fund-raiser fashion show in the Wall Street area where the girls were the guests of honor. They got all glammed up and took a stretch limo (courtesy of Kristin) to the Broad Street Ballroom, which is a gorgeous event space in an old bank. That wasn't all; there was a step-and-repeat wall where the girls had their photos taken and gave interviews.

Sabella, who received an award at the fashion show that she described as "the time of my life," was the most affected by the event. While she already had confidence, Sabella lacked anywhere to project it. After that night, and through Kristin's continued guidance, she could envision a level of success beyond Brownsville, which dissipated the anger she had held on to for the last three years.

I am proud of the youth summits and these other initiatives, but conversations about self-esteem and identity can't be special events. If kids are really going to feel good about themselves and become thoughtful, responsible adults, they need to be talked to all . . . the . . . time. If I had to name one thing that I take the most pleasure and pride in at Mott Hall, it's just that—there are conversations happening everywhere, *all the time.*

The charter school where I did my residency during the New Leaders program was excellent in classroom management and assessments. I can't argue against the fact that its data-centered approach improves test scores and keeps teachers accountable. But while I appreciated those strengths, I remember making a mental note that if I ever opened up my own school, I wouldn't have rules that made it so kids couldn't walk and talk in the hallway. On the way to my office, I'm energized hearing Mr. McLood talking with two eighth graders about what they are going to wear to the prom; my assistant principal, Mrs. Cadogan, having a philosophical discussion with another scholar about the purpose of writing down one's feelings and thoughts ("Is it for you or for other people?"); and my sixth-grade English language arts teacher, Ms. Kinsale, asking a scholar what the Animal Rescue Club is all about. The interchange of ideas and opinions can't be relegated to the classroom or formal extracurricular activities. That's not how it works in regular life.

Being dedicated to talking to children, however, means investing just as much time and energy in the unpleasant conversations as you do in the positive, happy ones. If not more.

There are children who I tend to defend more than others—to the point where I'm accused of favoritism. Antonne was a classic example. It wasn't that I liked him better than any other child. It was that I recognized there isn't a level playing field, even among the scholars at Mott Hall. Some kids simply arrive with more challenges that they have no control over.

Charles was another such kid. He was a lanky boy, so boisterous he couldn't keep his long limbs still for more than a minute, always looking for attention, even if it was of the negative variety, which it mostly was. He drove my staff nuts by shaking and shimmying, wearing his backpack on his stomach, and other incessant acts of goofiness. As I heard a teacher implore him, "Charles, just breathe in and out and don't do anything else!"

What I call goofy, however, others were more likely to describe as flamboyant. The other kids thought Charles, whose favorite activity was drawing fashions in his sketchbook, didn't act the way a boy should. Apparently so did his grandmother, as I learned when she came in for a meeting. As Charles's guardian, whom he lived with, she didn't want her grandson drawing fashion or doing dance, because she considered these things too effeminate. In the same conversation, the grandmother said that she had asked Charles if he wanted her to treat him "as a boy or a girl" but went on to explain that if he were gay she wouldn't want him in her house. I tried to get her to see how she was contradicting herself and setting up a scenario where Charles didn't really have a choice. Her only response was "Well, he really respects you."

"He doesn't want me," I said. "He wants you."

So, yes, I did think Charles had a particularly hard set of challenges before him, and I provided him with extra support by doing things like housing his sketchbook at school so he didn't have to bring it home, as well as letting him stay late so he could draw. While I was willing to give him the love he might not be getting at home, I was also there to put him in his place the minute he crossed the line.

When I found out that Charles had sparked a fight by taunting Malik for being too "stupid" and "old" for sixth grade, I was furious. Calling both boys into my office, I did not mince words about why I was particularly angry with Charles for hurling cruel comments at another scholar.

"I provide an open space for you to do something of interest to you without anyone judging you, and this is how you behave? How late did you stay here Friday night, drawing? Huh?"

Charles, who kept his eyes averted, didn't answer.

"I'm over here, Charles. It was eight P.M. before you left to go home. So how dare you try to ridicule someone for his age? He shows up here every day and spoke up when he needed help. That takes a lot. You, on the other hand, we have to sit with, coddle, create spaces for. You think that's okay? I'm over here, Charles.

"You boys put each other down when there is a whole

world out there to put you down. Hurt people are hurt people, and ya'll keep hurting each other— Hello! Uncross your arms please . . . So how do we resolve this?"

I was looking for Charles to apologize to Malik, but all I got was silent attitude. Now he was pushing *my* buttons.

"Charles, you aren't fixing your mouth to say something?"

Silence.

"I'm sorry, sir, you have nothing to say to Malik?"

More silence.

With still no apology coming from Charles, I turned to Malik and said, "Whether he accepts it or not, I need you to be the bigger person. There will be a hundred Charleses who will try to drag you down. I believe in you; you are intelligent. So you remember that, sir."

After Malik had left my office, I returned to Charles, who continued to look past me. These children are tough, but I'm tougher.

"Charles, you better face me . . . Do you think what you did is fair? . . . Use the words, yes or no.

"I'm the one person who really, really wants you to win, and you drag me into this? It tells me that you don't care, and that is selfish."

The boy refused to look at me, so I decided to stand close to him. Still he kept trying to avert his eyes. Every time he did, I moved into his line of vision. He was going to have to face me. I had a feeling that Charles hadn't lashed out at Malik for no reason. Most likely he had been provoked. But even if someone had called him a name, I was still angry that he had retaliated instead of coming to me or another adult so we could put an end to it. As I had said to him earlier, hurt people are hurt people.

"Someone making fun of you, and you aren't going to tell anyone? Did you tell Ms. Lopez? No. I went to bat with your grandmother. When you couldn't walk into your home, I spoke on your behalf. So how dare you not trust me when someone in your classroom is bothering you? You didn't tell me nothing, so I blame you.

"You do understand that?" I said.

Finally Charles spoke.

"Yes."

Just one word, but it was enough.

"You need to use your voice to tell someone. You also need to use your voice to apologize to me, but I don't want it right now because it has to be sincere, and I don't believe an apology from you right now would be sincere. When you are in other people's spaces where you are honored, you need to honor those spaces."

Although he still wouldn't look at me, tears started to roll down his face. I offered him a tissue, but he refused to take it. Defiance knows no bounds. So I wiped his face for him, shoved the tissue into his hands, and turned to my computer to do some work. We remained in silence for about ten minutes, with me working and him sitting, until I leaned in, touching my head to his, and talked softly.

"I need you to start acting like the scholar that I know you are."

Charles hung his head low.

"Are you hungry?" I asked.

These conversations aren't easy—and they aren't quick. People who visit Mott Hall always remark on the fact that I'm willing to spend a lot of time getting to the bottom of an issue with a scholar, teacher, or both. It's nothing for me to have a talk that takes an hour or more. One observer likened me to a detective, going around and around the "facts" until I get real answers.

I recognize that not everyone has the patience for this kind of work. Funny enough, it was my experience working at Verizon—what I did before going into education—that makes me uniquely qualified for this aspect of the job. At the phone company, I was part of a special team that dealt with the most irate customers, who had filed complaints with the Public Service Commission. Not only did I learn the art of managing people in their angriest states, but I also did extensive investigations.

A detective was what I became at Mott Hall after two female interns approached me in clear distress because a group of scholars had started a rumor that they had gone on a date with each other where they kissed. The young interns—who although they were pursuing their master's degrees in education while working at the school also volunteered their time to coach the softball team—felt violated by the scholars' casual cruelty.

I lined up all six girls who had been part of the gaggle and asked each of them over and over to explain who had started this rumor and why.

"I'm over this way . . .

"You've never had run-ins with me; you want to minimize that.

"Why is it nobody can seem to remember the name of this 'somebody' who started the rumor?"

While the two interns sat stony faced and looking out the windows, I continued with my inquiry.

"I'm disgusted by this behavior," I said. "You have two adults who come here and stay after hours and make sure you have someone to coach you in softball. You wouldn't have a team without them. One of you is going to get suspended, because this is slander. You could jeopardize their positions here. I don't even need to have another team. I'm saddened because we are the only school in this district that has a softball team. To be on sports, you have to have sportsmanship and be trustworthy. There are consequences to your actions. Do you understand? I need words."

"Yes," all the girls but one said, a detail that I did not fail to notice.

"I don't take things like this lightly," I said. "You are going to get to a place in your life where someone will say something about you that isn't true and can damage your reputation. When it's someone you know doing it, that really hurts."

I asked the interns if there was something they wanted to say. After hearing me talk for almost an hour, they had decompressed and were ready.

"I'm hurt. I don't think you understand that I can't talk I'm so hurt," one of them said. "What have I ever done to you for you to make up something like that? I help you with math. I intervene on your behalf with other teachers. Everything you want, I figure it out. I drop everything to make sure you are having fun and getting what you need."

The other intern, looking directly at the one girl who hadn't replied yes to my question, said, "When your classmates are dropping your name, the first thing I say is, 'Don't talk about her like that.' The one instance where you could have had my back, you didn't."

The girl started crying; everyone else stared at her in silence.

This may seem like harsh treatment for girls who fundamentally weren't thinking about the importance of their words. But my girls don't have the luxury of speaking without thinking. They will be judged throughout their lives for everything that comes out of their mouths.

I would rather they learn at Mott Hall, a place where they are truly loved and where they ultimately *always* get a second chance, the right way to treat those who care about them. These are the fundamental building blocks of success.

"I don't know where you all get off asking adults questions about their personal lives," I said. "You aren't here for that. You are children. I'm telling you what my expectations are: from now to the point you graduate, you don't ask any adult any question you wouldn't ask Ms. Lopez. In this school, gossip is not tolerated, just as bullying is not tolerated. To me all of you are the 'somebody' who started this because you all entertained it. You become either an up-stander or a bystander."

By the time the girls had filed out (two hours after we'd started), the interns were relieved. The intern who had singled out the girl who really hurt her had come in sullen but was now gregarious. "I'm not going to stop talking to her," she said, before launching into a lengthy monologue about how the girl is a natural athlete. "Yeah," the other intern agreed. "I'm not giving up on them. I just have to get them to make smarter decisions."

"They don't have boundaries in their own world, and they project that world onto here," I said of the scholars. "You always have to check them and say, 'I'm not your peer. You can't talk to me like that.'"

The interns both nodded, but I knew that the scholars

had found a chink in their armor and taken advantage of it. We talked about what had given rise to the girls talking about the interns' love lives. As it turned out, one of the girls had overheard an intern talking about what she was going to wear that night and asked if she had a date. When the intern responded with a nervous laugh, that was all it took.

"They don't want to analyze a text," I said about the kids, "but they can analyze *that*."

CHAPTER SIX

EXPANDING HORIZONS

I was forever changed during my first year of teaching in Fort Greene, when Ms. DeCoteau opened my eyes to the truth that children absorb many important lessons simply by getting out of their everyday surroundings. While walking across the Brooklyn Bridge with our class, I witnessed firsthand the power of experiential learning. That moment was the inspiration for Mott Hall's community walks, which have been part of the fabric of our school since the beginning. We leave Brownsville and travel to other communities so the scholars can learn that there's a much bigger world beyond the boundaries of their neighborhood—and that they have a place in it.

With television and the Internet, it's not as if my children aren't keenly aware that there is a whole other universe of privilege, wealth, and white people in America.

But it's one thing to watch people order lattes on TV and a whole other thing to actually sit in a café sipping a drink.

Getting outside the school building has long been considered a vital didactic tool for all students. The concept of the field trip is at the heart of experiential learning, a major trend in progressive education. It's the idea that people often learn best through experience, in other words, by doing things, going places, and making discoveries with their own eyes.

Yet more often than not children in underserved communities aren't offered these types of experiences. It's a huge injustice that the very students who stand to benefit the most from opportunities to expand what they've seen and done are precisely the ones denied them.

I first had this shocking revelation during my last year at Susan S. McKinney. After teaching at the Fort Greene middle school for two years, I had hit my stride. My students grew to such a level that they were engaged in a multidisciplinary project on Hurricane Katrina that encompassed discussions of not only political process and civil rights history but also global warming and the science behind its impact on weather. Just by coincidence, Al Gore's documentary *An Inconvenient Truth* hit the theaters at the same time we were working on this project. Honestly, I didn't even make the connection. It was my students—*my inner-city, special ed middle schoolers from the projects*—who brought the film to my attention. "Ms.

Lopez, we want to go and see it!" they said. It was the perfect field trip; the documentary would complement what they were learning in class as well as bring them into a current national conversation. I was so proud.

But when I asked the coordinator in charge of granting permission for field trips, he told me flat out, "No." If I wanted to show them the movie, he said, I could show them the bootleg version in school. *What?* I was so confused I didn't even get upset. I wasn't asking to take them to Great Adventure (which, by the way, I think is a great field trip, particularly when the theme park is free on Pi Day). This was directly connected to my students' work—not to mention that showing a bootleg version of a copyrighted movie is a federal offense.

"Do you understand you're actually asking me to commit a crime?" I said.

He just looked at me and said, "Well, these kids wouldn't even understand the movie."

Okay, *now* I was mad.

We never got permission to see *An Inconvenient Truth* as a class, which I tried to use as a teachable moment with my students. "Unfortunately there are those in this building who don't see the significance of you going on this trip and don't believe that you have the ability to understand the content in the film," I told them. "Sometimes in life there are going to be people who don't think you're capable and don't have expectations of you." But I encouraged them to expect more of themselves and, in this case, to ask their parents to take them to see the movie. Two out of a class of twenty-four students went. But if that was disheartening, it was nothing compared to what I felt when the same administrator shut my kids out of a college fair held at the school.

I can't stress enough the importance of events such as middle school, high school, and college information fairs for students like the ones at McKinney and Mott Hall. These children have been brainwashed into thinking that college is some prestigious, prohibitively expensive place they are totally unequipped to attend. While my immigrant parents couldn't tell me about college, they didn't come with the historical baggage that kept me from it either. So when I saw college as it was portrayed on the TV show *A Different World* I said to myself, "I'm going to college," and no one told me anything different or discouraged me. It wasn't that I thought college made you smarter, but I understood that you met people there you would never have met otherwise and that college gave you access to things my parents couldn't. Even *Chariots of Fire* was an inspiration. "I don't know if I'm going to do running," I said. "But college, yes."

My students at McKinney didn't have that internal confidence, and they certainly had no external encouragement, so the fair where they could get practical information on what it would take to make it to college, and encouragement that with hard work they would make it, was vital to them. When I told my kids we were going to attend the fair and get information that we'd go through together as a class, they got so excited.

As we moved from first period to second on the day of the fair, then to third and so on, I could feel their excitement mounting. Finally it was lunchtime, when I had promised we would attend the fair. But when we got downstairs, there were only two schools left from the thirty that had participated.

"Where are the schools?" I asked the coordinator.

"They're done," he said.

"Why didn't you tell me? I told you I wanted my kids to go to the fair."

"Ms. Lopez, like your kids are really going to go to college."

I lost it. I really did. How someone like that got into education and was able to exert that much control was beyond me.

Unfortunately, this wasn't my last time dealing with adults in schools who didn't believe in kids. In the year I spent as assistant principal of the middle school in P.S. 73 in Brownsville, I got a real understanding of why this community doesn't thrive. There were some angels, but mostly the school was populated with individuals hardened from years of no one listening to them. People walked around disheartened all day long; there was just no sense of trust.

College? Sure, statistically speaking, these kids are lucky to get all the way through high school, but that is no excuse for eliminating that dream, that expectation, from them at the start. At P.S. 73, there were not enough adults talking to kids about aspiring to anything beyond the school's walls or being better in any way. Far too many of the staff were all about clocking in, getting only the work required of them done, leaving, and that was it.

That was why the children in the Brownsville middle school reflected back exactly what was expected of them. They would leave rooms in total chaos. Lunchtime was war. The cafeteria was a series of little alcoves (basically holes in the wall) without windows. Crammed into the tight space, the students became restless, and lunch quickly devolved into the food fight scene from *Animal House*. It didn't matter what was served; if there were carrots, they would throw carrots. If they had chicken, they threw chicken. It was out of control.

In a vicious circle, the children's behavior seemed to reinforce the reason that P.S. 73 didn't offer any mentoring programs ("It won't make a difference with these kids"). So there were no college fairs; there weren't even trips to high schools. The result was that even the school's most promising students applied only to high schools in the immediate area, which were either subpar or failing.

That might have been okay for others at P.S. 73, but it wasn't okay with me. While I was there, two high-achieving eighth-grade students and best friends, Keandra and Eve, applied to high schools, and I made sure they set their sights higher than what was offered in Brownsville.

I had invested a lot in both of these girls because they were self-motivated and eager to take every opportunity that came their way. On Sundays I would drive from Crown Heights to retrieve Keandra and Eve from their houses in Ocean Hill and take them to meetings held by the incomparable Michaela Angela Davis. A former top editor at both *Essence* and *Honey* magazines, she is a writer, thinker, and activist on a wide variety of topics, from fashion to gender and race. She was also a mentor to a phenomenal group of women in their early twenties, who gathered every Sunday at Michaela's house for what she called Salon du Shine. Listening to those women talk about their passions and struggles in breaking into tough industries like fashion, entertainment, and journalism, Keandra and Eve received a different kind of education than the one they got at school. And so the two girls (and my daughter, Cenné) would come with me every single time Michaela had an event.

The investment wasn't wasted on them. Keandra was the salutatorian, and Eve only missed salutatorian by a couple of points. More important, the best friends were both accepted at Benjamin Banneker Academy, a public high school in Clinton Hill that boasted an academically rigorous program, which included courses of study including preengineering and communications as well as Advanced Placement courses.

Despite her high grade point average, Eve initially wasn't considered because she'd had so many absences during her seventh-grade year. But the numbers on her record didn't explain what had really happened. She had broken her ankle, and she lived on the seventh floor of one of the projects where the elevator wasn't working for more than three months, causing her to miss a whopping thirty-four days of school. During that time, though, she did all her work and passed all her exams. The principal of Banneker, Majida Abdul Karim, and I had a conversation where I explained the story behind the stats. Because I vouched for Eve, the principal accepted her. Eve's mom was my biggest fan. "Thank you, Ms. Lopez, for making it all possible for her," she said. "We love you."

But only three months into her freshman year of high school, Eve called me to say, "I can't stand it here. There's nobody else from Brownsville. And I don't understand anything I'm doing. I want to go to Transit Tech."

"I'm sorry. What?"

Having taken the call on my cell while I was driving, I was so upset I had to pull over. Eve wanted to leave a top New York City public high school to go to the vocational high school in East New York, which was not considered a competitive high school.

"Eve, you're not going to transfer to another high

school," I said. "You only want to go there because all the other kids from your middle school went there. You're not going to high school to be with friends. You're going to high school because you're going to go to college."

"It's so, like, uncomfortable there," she said.

My heart went out to her. She wasn't lazy or small-minded or incapable. Eve was human and feeling the pain of struggle. Not only was she dealing with the transition from middle school to high school but she was doing it in a place that felt totally foreign. Still, the way I could love her best was by not letting her give up.

"You and Keandra, being the first ones from Browns-ville, you're opening up doors. So when somebody else applies from Seventy-Three, and they see you walking those halls, they'll know that they belong. I'm not even staying on this phone. Okay? I'm going to call your principal. I'm going to find you people who are going to support you. Because you leaving is not an option."

As soon as I hung up with Eve I was on with her principal. "I need people to support her," I said. "She's not going anywhere else."

"I got you. That's not a problem," said Majida, who was also a friend, and she was true to her word. Eve graduated from Banneker and ended up attending the College of Staten Island. (Keandra went to college as well.)

It's amazing to think that a few phone calls changed the trajectory of Eve's life. The intervention her principal at Banneker and I provided didn't mitigate the fact that she had to do the work, make new friends, and have strength to be a trailblazer, but it gave Eve the *opportunity* for success.

Despite Eve's example, hope was in short supply at P.S. 73, particularly since most of the students didn't have the grades or ability of an Eve or a Keandra to follow through. It was for these kids that I asked Marlon Peterson, a good person I knew from growing up with him in Crown Heights who had just been released from prison, to help me out. "You have to come to my school. Every Friday," I said to him shortly after his release in 2009. "You're going to run a group for boys."

Not only were the boys at P.S. 73 in desperate need of a peer program with a mentor who had faced things they would most likely encounter, but also I knew Marlon would be great at providing it. Although he had spent a decade in prison for being an accessory to a botched robbery in which the assailants, who got life in prison, murdered two people, Marlon had already been helping me with my kids for years. In 2003, when I was teaching at McKinney, I sent him a letter in which I talked about my kids in Fort Greene, who lacked guidance and often made unhealthy decisions. Because he was a good kid from a good family, who had wound up in the wrong place with the wrong people, I knew he would understand. I asked if he would be willing to correspond with them. After getting clearance from the principal, Marlon and my students wrote letters back and forth almost every week, which I reviewed before they were distributed.

I always knew Marlon was thoughtful, but I was bowled over by the depth of feeling in his letters as he wrote about how his loss of freedom affected his being. In turn, I sent him *Understanding by Design,* a seminal book on how to design curriculum by Jay McTighe and Grant Wiggins, with the exhortation "When you come out you're going to create your own program and go into schools to help kids in underserved communities understand how to stay out of prison."

Marlon took to education like a fish to water. While still in prison, he participated in Two Communities Bridging the Gap, a program facilitated by Vassar College that brought students from the college, in Poughkeepsie, New York, and incarcerated people together to discuss social justice through experiential learning.

Vassar, one of the country's most elite private colleges, has a history of offering programs for incarcerated populations, including a community reentry course, which started when Lawrence Mamiya, a veteran of the civil rights movement and professor of religion and African studies, began a dialogue between Vassar students and inmates at an upstate prison back in the seventies.

When Marlon got out of prison, he met with about twenty boys at P.S. 73 every single Friday. He went on to found the Precedential Group, an organization to reduce gun violence in Brooklyn. Vassar was sufficiently impressed with his work in and out of jail to extend the opportunity for him to bring students from our school to the college for a visit. He said if I could find the means of getting them to Poughkeepsie, he'd love to do it. The principal agreed it was worth the price of a bus to give thirty kids the opportunity to visit an elite college. Her opinion was the only one that mattered, but nobody else agreed with her.

The other adults in the building were so negative about the trip that I decided I didn't want any of them to go on it. I didn't need that kind of energy coming along. However, I did let the teachers select which students to go on the trip—that is, all but one.

I had decided as soon as the principal gave the go-ahead that Kyle—who had been suspended for two months after threatening Mr. Principal, at the time a math teacher at P.S. 73—had to go. Although everyone had counted him out, Kyle was smart. But with a mother who couldn't manage him, he was growing up with gangs. The teachers were up in arms when I added him to the list. Why was I rewarding someone so defiant and beyond hope? What kind of message did that send to the other students?

"This is about opportunity. You can pick thirty students, but he will be going."

From the moment the bus pulled out at 7:30 in the

morning until we arrived, Kyle was quiet, staring out at the greenery, rapt the way my McKinney students had been at the sight of the river after our Brooklyn Bridge crossing. Only once, when we neared Poughkeepsie, did Kyle take off his headphones and, without taking his eyes off the land, ask me, "Where are we?"

"Dutchess County," I said.

"There's like cows and stuff; and there's so much grass."

"Yeah."

Walking the college grounds was an epiphany. That alone would have made the two-hour trip worth it. The kids were awed by the perfectly manicured quad, stately buildings, and students walking around with books and purpose. That, however, was just the start. Our first stop was a meeting with Kiese Laymon, a talented writer born and raised in Jackson, Mississippi, and an associate professor of English at Vassar. If seeing a black college professor who looked just like them wasn't empowering enough, Kiese began by saying, "We're going to do an assignment."

There was a bunch of grumbling from the kids: "Assignment? We didn't come to work."

"You all didn't even think I was a college professor, right?" he challenged them. "Why? Because I wear Air Force 1, jeans, and a jacket? That don't take anything away from it. I'm just like you. I wasn't born rich. But I went to school. So we're going to do this assignment.

"Write a sentence or two about what you saw walking on the college campus."

After they wrote their sentences, he said, "Now what I want you to do is look at your sentences again and, using your five senses, add description—whether it's a color, a sound, a smell, how something felt to the touch. I want you to add that."

The kids did as they were told. When they were done, Kiese added another layer. "Think about the feelings behind the experience; I want you to write that into it," he said.

By the time they were done, most of the students, even those who typically struggled with writing, had written a paragraph that represented some of their best work.

Kiese had many of them read their work out loud and offered comments on what he liked from their descriptions and insights. "This is a college 101 class assignment," he said. "And you all did excellent. So how many of you are going to college?"

Only two of the thirty-one hands went up.

"Why aren't you going to college?"

Edgar, a Dominican kid who loved to play baseball, raised his hand: "I don't have the money."

"How many of you feel like this young man?" Kiese asked.

Every hand went up at the same time.

"There is no reason you can't make it to college," he said, before explaining to them about college endowments that offer scholarships. "If it's not here, it needs to be somewhere. You can go to a city college; you can go to a state college. But don't ever let the money stop you from getting where you need to be. This *can* be an option.

"The next time somebody asks you if you want to go to college, what are you going to say?"

"We're going to go," they shouted.

"Great. My work is done."

And that was just forty-five minutes of our trip! After the class, we did a tour of the campus on which we got to see the dorms. "What's dorms?" the kids asked. After I explained that they were where students lived during the school semester, they couldn't believe it. "You get to live here? Who pays the rent?" There was so much that they didn't know. The cafeteria was another place of amazement. "We get to choose? You get to just pick? You can go back as many times as you want? Nobody's going to tell you no?"

When we boarded the bus to return home, Kyle turned to me and with all seriousness said, "Ms. Lopez, I need you to understand something. I'm going to college. I don't care where, when, how. I'm going to go."

Back at school, the kids who had been to Vassar didn't stop talking about this idea of what they could achieve, how they were going to college, what their rooms would be like. But the person the trip had the greatest effect on, hands down, was Kyle.

The student who had threatened Mr. Principal walked into the math teacher's room the day after the trip and said, "What do I need to do to graduate?"

Mr. Principal was taken aback, but Kyle proved he was serious. He came before school, worked through lunch, and stayed after school. When his old friends would try to get him to roll, he stayed focused. "I ain't going nowhere," he said. "I'm getting my work done." Kyle finished every single thing. And he graduated—not just middle school but high school as well. I lost touch with him after that, but before he went on the field trip, Kyle most likely would have dropped out and, statistically speaking, been headed for jail.

That a two-hour trip upstate for one day could change the trajectory of a child's entire life only served to strengthen the conviction I developed after walking across the Brooklyn Bridge with Ms. DeCoteau. On Mott Hall's community walks we stick closer to home—hopping on the subway to visit other parts of Brooklyn, like Park Slope or Williamsburg—but the dichotomy between Brownsville and these other neighborhoods is just as startling. Like Kyle on the bus to Poughkeepsie, the scholars who act out in school or in their neighborhood get real quiet on these walks. In their observations of the shops, restaurants, beautiful homes, and people of different ethnicities, they feel outnumbered.

In Brownsville there is no diversity, no gentrification

happening yet. So they don't have to assimilate to anything else. They're in the majority, and they act in accord with their majority. They want to challenge authority, challenge their peers. They just want to challenge, challenge, challenge. But they won't do that outside of their community, where they notice things such as the fact that there are restaurants where you can actually sit down and eat instead of just take out. That leads to a discussion about how, in these neighborhoods, restaurants are for when people want to commune over a meal. Where they come from, there are no restaurants for families to sit and eat together. In cafés, they are shocked that a cup of coffee costs three dollars, because in Brownsville it's fifty cents. But, as I explain, there's no free Wi-Fi or place to work on your laptop at the corner store.

In these places that have so much more than their neighborhood does, my scholars are reminded of all the things they are *not*. "I don't look like these people. I don't talk like them. I don't have money like them. They are smarter than me." The conclusion of all these thoughts is: "I'm not valuable enough to be here."

This dynamic is part of the conversation in African American communities as a symptom of post-traumatic slave syndrome. There is an aspect of being appeasing and subservient when we are in spaces where we're not dominant. It's destructive to the psyche and precisely why I bring the students into places that feel foreign to them.

To help them understand their confusing feelings, we always have a debriefing after our community walks where we talk about the places they visited and process the differences they noted. I'm not looking for them to get past their feelings, but I want them to build up their self-awareness. Not only do I question them on what their lives might look like if they had access to the same kinds of amenities that exist in, say, Park Slope, but also I urge them to better understand how they are shaped by *their* community. What does it mean when you grow up in a place that has a jail for juveniles smack in the middle of the neighborhood?

Ultimately, though, I put my scholars in these uncomfortable situations because the more they are in them, the more they will become used to them—and comfortable. "Why can't you walk down these blocks?" I ask them. Yes, my scholars need to know how to "code-switch," that is, to be authentic in their community but to conduct themselves in a different manner when they step outside. I don't sugarcoat it with my kids; if they don't learn to code-switch, they will be perceived at best as unintelligent and at worst as threats. All of this, no doubt a great challenge, begins with them believing they belong in any neighborhood they choose to go to. "Stop being insignificant in this space," I say.

I want this community to know that they deserve more. There are amenities close by, and they have as much right to enjoy them as anyone else. I want my scholars to know they can get on a subway and go to a museum, Central Park, or Barnes & Noble—*especially* Barnes & Noble, because there are no bookstores around Brownsville. As far as they're concerned, bookstores are in the city—or there's one on Court Street. But if my scholars are going all the way to Cobble Hill, three neighborhoods away from Brownsville (or wherever), it's to go to the movies at the multiplex, not the bookstore. Why would they want to go to a bookstore? For them, bookstores are not places to have fun or a great experience, and not places they feel particularly welcomed.

There aren't even newsstands in Brownsville. The *New York Times* does not exist in this neighborhood. I've gone into the corner store near Mott Hall and asked if they get the newspaper delivered, and their response is "For what? People around here don't even read." There is no encouragement for reading whatsoever.

Even the public library on the corner of Mother Gaston Boulevard and Dumont Avenue is hidden in plain sight. That's because there is *no* significant sign outside the historic Stone Avenue Branch, the 1914 Andrew Carnegie building that was the first freestanding children's library. The library is still stunning, inside and out, mainly because people don't really take advantage of it. When you go inside, the books look untouched. Most of my boys at Mott Hall couldn't come to the library anyway, because it's outside their turf.

Any books my scholars get at school are required reading for class, since, like more and more New York City public schools, we don't have a library. Due to budget cuts; the creation of smaller schools (like Mott Hall), whose enrollment falls below the state's minimum requirement for funding a school librarian; and the idea that technology can supplant books on a shelf, the number of school libraries in New York City has plunged from 1,500 in 2005 to 700 in 2014. And the libraries that *do* exist don't all have librarians.

When I was a child, not only did I have a library card but the library, a friendly place, was around the corner from my house. And my parents, who bought me books regularly, had a small library of their own at home. Once I got to high school and was taking the train up to Harlem every day, I became fascinated with how people reading the *New York Times* folded the paper in such a way that they could hold on to the straps and still read, and I knew I had to learn that skill.

My scholars don't have any of that. Their parents, who have just as little access to books, don't keep libraries at home, read to their children, or buy their kids books they might like. Books are textbooks they get at school and have nothing to do with pleasure. It's no wonder then that children in Brownsville don't read on grade level.

When Kincade, one of my scholars, who had a talent for design and an uncanny European sense of personal style, was getting set to graduate from Mott Hall, I asked him if he had ever been to a bookstore. After he answered no, I told him we were going to the Barnes & Noble in Union Square.

His eyes widened when we walked into the chain's New York flagship store. "You all right?" I asked.

"I've never seen this many books," Kincade said, looking all around the soaring first floor.

"There are a lot more floors. Let's go," I told him.

We headed to the third floor, where I took him into the magazine section and started pulling titles. I found European versions of *GQ* and men's *Vogue* to show him the clothes that reminded me of his style.

"Oh, these are nice," he said.

"You're not going to find this in Brownsville."

Then we went to the other side of the floor, where I found a home design magazine with images of big, airy interiors, like one of a bedroom with a view of the ocean. "I'm getting you this because I want you to imagine where you should see yourself," I said. "I want you to have a vision of peace. Whenever you feel like, ugh—I want you to have this view."

Then I bought him a sketchbook in which to make drawings and paste images cut out from the magazines we had chosen. "This is an inspiration to remind you that everything you want, you can do," I said.

"All right, Ms. Lopez," Kincade replied.

"You are definitely going to become an outstanding gentleman," I said. And he has already been recognized for his artistic talents. Kincade was one of a small group of high schoolers selected by the Tribeca Film Institute to participate in a year-round fellowship program for young filmmakers.

It is good for everyone to get out of his or her comfort zone once in a while. Children aren't the only ones who benefit from having their perspectives widened. Part of my passion for networking with people whose backgrounds, professions, or viewpoints are often different from mine stems from the fact that I always get an education from those interactions. Even my teachers, these remarkable men and women who dedicate themselves to the exhausting, often thankless work of changing children's lives, need to be shaken up from time to time.

Not that I'm complaining about my teachers, who by the fourth year of the school, had become the cohesive group of motivated and thoughtful individuals I'd always hoped for. In addition to those already on staff, such as Ms. Achu, Mr. Principal, Mr. McLeod, and Coach Randy, we had added many other enthusiastic educators, like our phys ed teacher, Mr. Blake, who is passionate about our sports teams whether they win any games or not ("I'm not a gym teacher. Gym is a space. I am a physical education teacher," he said at his interview).

By supporting one another in their teaching practices,

the staff grew as a team. But I took their community building a step further by having the teachers engage in the hiring process, so that they would be invested in their colleagues' success from day one. When we are ready to bring in a new teacher, a committee of staff and teachers first goes through all the résumés and invites any qualified candidates to teach a demo lesson to an assorted group of scholars who offer a real taste of the school's population. The scholars' feedback is solicited as well (they have *no* problems giving their honest opinions). Based on the recommendations from my staff and scholars, I decide whether or not to meet with a candidate. The whole process serves as a great way to vet teachers for me. More important, however, when the teachers are included in the decision-making process of hiring someone new, they become accountable for that person's trajectory. We succeed or fail together.

Despite all that my teachers do day in and day out to improve the lives of the scholars, they still suffer from tunnel vision and take for granted the biases of their perspective. I was reminded of this on a hot day right before the summer break of 2014, when, as the teachers drifted into the classroom and took their seats for our weekly staff meeting, a few of them started complaining among themselves about the behavior of the kids, who were being especially bad.

I also wasn't in the best mood. My chronic case of summer anxiety was already coming on. The Sunday before, I had been returning from church through Brownsville, as I always do. I usually drive, but on this particular day, I decided to park my car and walk through the housing developments and surrounding city blocks. I grew more and more depressed as I passed the check-cashing stores, Chinese food joints, nail salons, Laundromats, and bodegas that sell beer at the front and Lotto tickets; once my scholars were on school vacation, there would be no safe spaces for them other than inside their apartments.

Listening to my teachers' gripes about the last days of school before their vacation, I realized that they needed to step out of their own perspective to see the fuller picture clearly.

All of us have our blind spots—even teachers, who are so involved in the lives of their students that they see things the parents of these children don't, like a scholar's ability in drawing or another's growing stomach, which she tries to hide from everyone, even herself. Yet our teachers' relationships with our scholars take place almost exclusively within the confines of Mott Hall. My teachers put in more than full days at school, but when they clock out, most of them get right into their cars and drive straight home, just like I do. They don't spend time hanging out in Brownsville, because not only would it most likely be dangerous but also there's nothing there.

I understood why my staff was ready for a vacation.

The end of the year is tough on everyone. Teachers are racing to finish up the curriculum. And after working hard all year long in a tough community, they are looking forward to time off to recharge. Unfortunately, our kids don't have the same luxury.

As much as I wanted my teachers to have the break they deserved, I also wanted them to remember that for our scholars there was no break from this reality. And that's when it dawned on me: my *teachers* needed to go on a community walk—through Brownsville.

At that meeting, I had initially planned to go over some recent data. Instead I gave the teachers an assignment to write about their favorite childhood vacation. Their faces lit up as they recalled fond memories. You should have seen the smiles during those five minutes they had to write them down.

When they were done, I asked them to pair up and discuss what they had written. The room was buzzing with stories of beaches, porches, a favorite mango tree.

"Great!" I said. "Now I want you to look to your left."

They looked to their left, out the line of gate-covered windows to where the housing projects loomed in the near distance.

"What do you think summer's like there?"

It was suddenly real quiet.

"You can't wait to get on that plane or drive to the beach; meanwhile our scholars will be home by themselves for hours at a time. And the only thing they'll be able to do is watch TV. There are no adults to talk to them. There are no peers that they can relate to. Sometimes what we provide them in terms of lunch and breakfast are the only meals they get.

"If you would say to the kids, 'I'm going to have class this summer,' they would be here. They would *all* be here. Especially the ones who act like they don't want to be here. They're anxious because summer is coming, but they don't know how to say, 'I'm anxious.'

"I want you to know what it feels like to be in Brownsville during the hot summer. No plane ticket, no nothing. So, this afternoon, we're going to walk."

We started by making our way through the Brownsville Houses, where the green spaces between the apartment buildings were empty. Nobody was sitting on the benches. "Why do you think that is?" I asked the teachers.

"It's not safe," one of them answered.

"Right. The intention in building this housing was to contain people, but safety was compromised. When you don't feel safe, there is always a feeling of hopelessness, because safety is the foundation for thriving. If you are constantly in a state of fear, you can't aspire to anything more than just surviving."

We crossed Mother Gaston Boulevard to the Van Dyke Houses. The door to Van Dyke's community center was locked; a sign stated that anyone entering must remove all headgear, including hoods and sunglasses. I noted to the teachers that we were now in the Van Dykes, but the difference didn't seem to make an impression. For our boys, most of whom have affiliations with gangs, the difference was everything. I got why the teachers didn't have a clue—the boys don't show they're on opposing teams in our school. Once they get outside, though, all bets are off.

"It's territory," I said. "Kids from Seth Low or Howard Houses can't come to this community center. It's a death sentence if they do. And the library? If you tell the kids they have to go to the library, some of them can't even cross over to go there, because then they would be traveling into another gang's area. We often don't think about those things."

Then we went by an elementary school whose fence around the courtyard playground was fifty feet high. "Where have you seen a fence like this? Just think."

"Prison," a few people answered. The answer was obvious. So much in this community—from the floodlights that come on at night to police kiosks that sit in the middle of the projects—is reminiscent of prison, as if its residents are constantly being taught to become inured to incarceration.

Another elementary school was embedded within the projects so that there was no delineation between the buildings the students live in, where people urinate in the elevators and broken locks don't get fixed, and school. Even the bricks were the same. "It's no wonder kids have trouble differentiating between their behavior at home and their behavior at school when they grow up seeing them as one and the same," I said.

Just then a fire engine sounded its siren. The wail was deafening because the Fire Department was adjacent to the elementary school. "Who did this?" I asked. "Who thought that this was a good idea to put a fire station right next to the school where kids are supposed to be learning?"

On the way to our next stop, a huge supermarket on Mother Gaston Boulevard, a pair of police helicopters suddenly swarmed overhead. The noise as they hovered above us was deafening and the air their propellers disturbed kicked up the trash from the ground. It felt more like Baghdad than Brooklyn. They were doing a sweep, looking for someone. Everyone on the street glanced up for a minute and then carried on with business, desensitized to the racket that jarred us but was commonplace to them. "Who's on the loose now?" an old-timer asked.

Inside, the vast, almost suburban-like supermarket was cool, and for a second the teachers felt some relief. That is, until I pointed out the cameras that were all around us. Every aisle we went down there was a line of cameras hanging above. In the front of the supermarket there was a camera about every two feet, and there were more around each cashier. I counted a total of at least thirty-two. "Can you imagine shopping here?" I asked my staff. "They have more cameras than Tiffany's." That's when one of my teachers remarked that nobody was in the store. It was indeed the emptiest supermarket I ever saw. Back outside we were greeted by the sight of a man urinating by the edge of a park where five little children were playing.

Often there is a disconnect between teachers who work in underserved communities and their students. Public school, charter school, it doesn't matter; many of those who come into the teaching profession think they are going to "save" kids. That is the biggest mistake. This is not a Third World country. This is real life in the United States of America, and the qualities in these kids that frustrate teachers are the very same ones that help them survive every day.

These children—accustomed to adult responsibilities, abandonment, and a general state of not having—are hustlers. With parents who have the responsibility of work or lack the capacity to take care of children, our scholars are caregivers for themselves and siblings—a role they put all of themselves into. In order to get from school to their homes alive, often with little ones in tow, they need to ignore many adults along the way. When they come to school, they don't know how to shift to being children. On an unconscious level, they don't understand that a teacher is a different kind of adult, one they should obey. They can't turn off those thoughts that say, *No one is there to take care of me, so I run my own ship, and I don't need to listen to you.*

Teachers react by running through the whole gamut of negative feelings: "They're rude; they're disrespectful. They're just downright nasty. They don't want to focus. They don't want to listen." That is a part of what accounts for the high turnover rate of teachers in poorer schools. The satisfaction of helping a child expand his or her potential isn't easy, immediate, or obvious.

The teachers at Mott Hall understand this dynamic either because they come from disadvantaged communities like Brownsville themselves or because we talk about it all the time at school. Still, understanding doesn't make it any easier when a child is cursing you out in the classroom. Feeling hurt and concluding that the child is ungrateful is a perfectly natural response. The only way I can keep my teachers working with the intensity and compassion they do no matter how bad the kids get is by reminding them, through exercises like our Brownsville walk, *why* the kids are bad.

The poverty and lack of opportunity our scholars live with create a hunger for power. In a place where everyone is struggling, the question becomes "What can you really control?" In an attempt to feel better-than and to have a sense of power, my scholars resort to what they know, as we all do. It's just that what they know is fighting. They can't conceive of a life without violence. They understand the immediate fear and threat of the street but don't fear the more distant but very real possibility of losing everything if they don't get with the system. They don't understand that this is not what it's like outside of Brownsville, and they don't see the effects of their confrontational behavior in a wider context—namely, how fighting negates everything about their intelligence and abilities.

Destroying yourself or your peers doesn't help get you out of the place that is keeping you down. That is why I'm always asking them what their legacy will be. It's an attempt to get them to see past their immediate situation and forecast into the future, where being violent will keep them from going to college, running a business, or owning an apartment.

As much as they act like they don't want discipline and consistency, our children actually do. Like I say to them, "I know y'all are tough, but as long as you know someone cares about you, you don't have to worry about who doesn't like you and you don't have to fight. I want you to have real choices in your life."

And though they'll give a teacher so many problems in class, the minute that teacher is absent they want to know, "Where have you been?" Even that kid who is the bane of your existence will be concerned. They won't necessarily express it in words, but you'll see a difference when you're back. My scholars are always keeping tabs on my whereabouts; sometimes if I'm holed up in my office and don't make it down the hallway, the children will check me on it. "Ms. Lopez, you have to do better," they'll say in all seriousness. That's why I always try to make sure I say, "Good morning," to every scholar every day. If they don't see me for the rest of the day, they're fine. But if I don't check in at all, they aren't happy at all.

The idea of *saving* kids hints at trying to change them or remove them from their situation. That's not the approach we take at Mott Hall. We *aren't* taking them *out of* Brownsville, so the only thing we can do is drill down into who they are as human beings and how they can achieve *in* Brownsville. Appreciation, although not assured, is more likely to come when a kid feels you really care about who he is as a person and don't see him as a charity case. Children are in tune with who's there for them and who's not—and they make that understanding very clear.

As the teachers and I finished our walk, I said, "So this is their summer. It's hot. And there's nothing that reminds them of being really great, nothing for them to be active and productive. Instead they get into fights and kids get killed. It's why they come back in the fall and know absolutely nothing. Because they're just trying to survive. That's it."

The next day I posted pictures of our walk on the outside of my door for the scholars to see.

"What's this, Ms. Lopez?" they asked.

"Yesterday the teachers had to go on a walk."

"They went on a walk?"

"Yup. They took a tour of Brownsville."

As it registered with the scholars that the teachers were being schooled in something *they* knew well—their stories, their neighborhood—they began nodding their heads and smiling, like, "Now they know how we live!"

My staff felt similarly grateful for the eye-opening experience, which I decided to make an annual event. Even my secretary, Ms. Marzano, a woman who didn't put up with a whole lot no matter the excuse, was moved by what she'd seen on our tour. "I want to thank you for feeling like I should have been part of the walk," she said to me. "For all the time, you said, 'Carol, don't take it personally, they just have a lot going on,' it was walking around that did it. Now, I clearly understand the frustration that our families go through. And from now on when they call and are upset, I'm going to check in with them or at least give them a moment."

CHAPTER SEVEN

THE STRUGGLE OF LEADERSHIP

T here was a lot to be proud of when Mott Hall entered its fifth year, in the fall of 2014. As a complete sixth- through eighth-grade school, we had sent seventy-two of our seventy-five graduates to high schools outside Brownsville. We had also taken over the entire third floor of the school building. For the first three years of our existence, we only had three-quarters of the floor, which presented distractions during transitions between classes. The boundary of Mott Hall, previously just the third doorway from the last on the left-hand side, was now real and established—like us. We even had a student government, conceived of and created by the scholars, and a school magazine, *The Score: Brownsville Brilliance,* which they wrote, edited, laid out, and produced digitally.

Mott Hall was also written up in the *New York Times.*

The article from December of that year, entitled "A Brooklyn School's Curriculum Includes Ambition," described our school as "a safe zone in a crime-plagued neighborhood, and a gateway out of generational poverty for those born with few advantages in life." In the same article, the new chancellor for New York's public schools, Carmen Fariña, was quoted as saying, "Mott Hall Bridges Academy is proving that any school—no matter its ZIP code—can deliver a great education for its students." Yet the same article couldn't help but report that our scores on the state math and English tests were "well below the citywide average."

As much as I believed in the vision and mission of my school, I was stressed out about our numbers and told anyone who would listen that I lived in fear of them. I think I speak for every principal when I say that there is a never-ending fear that if your numbers don't meet expectations, you will be seen as a failure who didn't do what you needed to. No matter how much you try to argue the proficiency of your students as readers, mathematicians, scientists, and human beings; no matter how many articles are written about your school; no matter how happy the children and adults are working within its walls—if the state exam scores don't meet expectations, the response will be "Is she really preparing kids for college? Is she preparing them for a successful life?"

Even though I knew we had changed lives for the better

in the short time since Mott Hall had opened, introduced children to the love of learning and built their self-esteem to last long past middle school—I still felt pressure from not meeting the demands of a national education policy crafted in places far from Brownsville.

The Common Core State Standards, the national standards-based education reform, got its start in 2010, when a consortium of governors, corporate CEOs, and experts in education drafted a checklist of the academic skills they felt were necessary for high school graduates to make it in colleges and today's workforce. The standards they outlined cover what any student in the country should know in math and English language arts for each grade from kindergarten through twelfth—and forty-five states initially signed on to adopt them. As the Common Core rolled out across the nation, I wasn't sure we could attain what was being asked. I wasn't even sure *what* was being asked.

The Common Core Standards leave it up to the states and school districts to figure out what modes of study and materials conform to the standards. In the 2013–14 academic year, the second year New York State gave the new tests, the Department of Education recommended switching to a new set of Common Core textbooks, known as Expeditionary Learning. The new curriculum sounded really great, and it might have been well intended, but the textbooks didn't arrive until the week school started. The professional development programs led by the DOE over the summer were theoretical rather than practical because there weren't any actual texts the teachers could look at. But the essence of teaching is preparation. And my teachers had no time to prepare.

Instead, they were forced to process the new textbooks and how they interpreted the curriculum *while* they were teaching. The result was that, across the board, a unit took three months to get through when it should have taken six weeks. "How long are we going to be on this?" I begged. Even though I knew they were doing their best, every day we were falling more behind.

In addition, no one higher up takes into consideration what kids lack in the social skills that are required to navigate the real world. The system isn't designed to honor the intangibles that can't be quantified on a test. That's why, although I'm hard on my teachers, I am always mindful of their energy. I always tell them how much I appreciate them for being willing to work with one another, stay after school, and even come in on weekends. I also try to remind them that success isn't just excellence but growth.

No one takes it harder than teachers when their students don't do well on tests. When the state interim assessments scores came in, Mr. Principal put on his sourpuss face, and I called him into my office for a talk.

"Teaching is very personal. I put myself into my lessons and my work," he said. "When the results come out marred, how can I not take that very personally?"

I held up the scores from his scholars' assessments and pointed out a few students.

"Look at Jacqui," I said. "She came in scoring a twenty. A *twenty*. Now, look, she got a forty. That's meaningful. I know in your mind 'better' means eighties, nineties, or hundreds, but a difference is a difference. You are dealing with years of disservice in only a year or two, and yet the growth is noticeable. This is your hard work."

I meant the praise I offered my teachers, but I know I also instilled fear. Like so many other school leaders, I couldn't help but let my anxiety over testing trickle down to the teachers, from whom the fear about mastering material trickled down to the scholars. Teachers are in a race against time if they try to engage in a course of study that speaks to the actual children in their rooms as well as cover material that will help their students pass the exams. Further complicating matters is the instructional time that is lost to prepping and taking these tests, as well as the fact that the national and state approaches to quantifying students' academic abilities keep changing.

I never felt more anxiety than in the fall of 2013, when the textbooks came too late and I had to decide whether we should cut our losses and go back to the old books. If we went with the new material despite not being prepared to teach it and the kids didn't do well on the exams, it would be my fault. If we went back to our old textbooks, and the kids didn't do well because we used out-of-date resources, it would also be my fault.

In the end, I decided to go back to the old textbooks. I had to. We were falling so far behind my teachers were never going to make it through the basic units. I had no idea how our kids would do on the test. Everyone was stressed out. Who suffers the most from this scenario? The kids, of course.

They didn't do well on the tests. In the English language arts state assessments for 2013–14, 47 percent of my scholars were Level 2, "below proficient," and 35 percent were Level 1, "well below proficient." (Level 3 is proficient, and on Level 4 are students who excel.) A whopping 72 percent of my sixth-grade class scored 2s on the English language arts exam. Our overall math scores were almost equally dismal. And it wasn't just that the teachers didn't have enough time to prepare. The state exam didn't actually test the contents of the new textbooks. Whatever the reasons, it felt like an epic fail.

Perhaps it was defensiveness, but I wondered if the people who created this standards-based policy had spent time in real classrooms. The group of politicians, business leaders, and education experts was making such profound decisions that affected how we ran our schools it seemed only common sense for principals like me to understand the rationale behind their choices. I wasn't about to get an invitation to Washington anytime soon. But I knew for sure that unless you actually showed up to see a place like Mott Hall, it was unfair to knock us. That's a time-consuming and inefficient process, but there is no other way to understand why educators in underserved communities struggle.

People always wonder what I'm doing when they call or come in after hours, during vacations, or on the weekends and invariably find me here. I don't get paid to be here during those times; I do it because I want to. This is my calling in life. But I also do it because I need to. Because I have a responsibility. There's an expectation that, if you stop by the building, there will always be someone to talk to you. My scholars just want a space where they will be heard. If I'm not here, where else do they have to go?

Mott Hall is a nurturing environment where we give the scholars as much love and positive reinforcement as we can, not to soften them but to build up all those life skills they so desperately need to succeed when they leave us. Everything I wanted children to learn in our building—from respect for themselves to a strong work ethic—was to prepare them for the real world. While students in other districts might already have a foundation for communication, problem solving, conflict resolution, and so on, we have to spend so much time developing those basic life skills in our scholars. So much work has to be put into building a culture that bucks every negative stereotype associated with Brownsville. But when you walk into Mott Hall Bridges and find a bright environment with children learning, speaking, and smiling, you will instantly understand our efforts' worth.

The first test of the resiliency we try to build up in our scholars is immediate: high school. Once students are in high school—New York City public high school—there's not enough time in the day to address social, emotional, and even personal academic needs. It's every student for himself or herself. So high school students will either fall prey to someone who constantly reminds them that they're not good enough or ally themselves with individuals they can draw something from. My scholars will always have to maneuver through a society that tries to say they are insignificant, but they'll be able to stand up for themselves by replying, "You don't have that power over me."

Graduates always return to Mott Hall when they are off from school, primarily to get a little love. But when they stop by to chat, they tell me about high school and any problems they are having there. One of the most common is trouble finding teachers willing to give them additional instruction or guidance.

In high school, where there can be upward of two thousand kids, students have to be able to work independently. But part of working independently, as we teach them, is that when you don't know something, you ask for help.

What bothers me (although it doesn't surprise me) is how so many of my former scholars are turned away when they ask for that help.

That Mott Hall is an anomaly in an otherwise unforgiving system is a point I try to hammer home with all my scholars, just as I did with a group of sixth-grade boys dumped in my office for repeated bad behavior. "Listen to me, I have boys come here all the time that used to be just where you are, and I can report back that no one's going to love you all like we do," I said. "No one's going to talk to you all like we do. No one's going to make time. This is not your reality beyond Mott Hall. We do this because, if we don't do this for you now, you're going to be stuck for the rest of your lives."

And yet, we at Mott Hall aren't measured for the love we show our scholars. We aren't measured on any aspect of our culture. No one measured scholars' knowledge on Pointillism, medians, the last of the great Chinese dynasties, or how growing up a poor, black woman in the 1950s like Henrietta Lacks affects the course of your medical treatment. No one measured the ground we covered in the social emotional development of children. No one measured that a child who was angry was now smiling. No one measured the impact of a real estate agent mentoring a boy with an incarcerated father each and every week. No one measured how Ms. Dorn, the art teacher who once wanted to quit, was now so empowered in her job that she secured a twenty-thousand-dollar grant from the National Recreation and Park Association to create a garden that included solar panels.

I'm not against testing. In fact, I believe the city's interim assessments in the fall and spring are useful tools for figuring out what the kids know and what they don't know (and then teaching them what they don't know so they can catch up). I've trained all my teachers in data-driven instruction, by which they analyze the tests to see what the students' gaps in skills and knowledge are. Testing isn't bad if the tests have an unambiguous point.

There is no one who has higher standards for my scholars than me, but the problem with testing in its current form is that it continuously perpetuates the idea that the kids aren't achieving and aren't smart enough. The same children I watched have phenomenal conversations in our entrepreneurship class or dissect sheep brains, received 1s and 2s on state exams in math and English language arts, which require mastery of texts whose complexity and cultural references are beyond them—at least at this point in their lives.

(A widely ridiculed example from a 2015 ELA exam for sixth graders was a *Smithsonian* magazine piece entitled "Nimbus Clouds: Mysterious, Ephemeral and Now Indoors." The article, about the work of Dutch artist Berndnaut Smilde, which appeared in some versions of the test, contained language many adults would find convoluted:

"As a result, the location of the cloud is an important aspect, as it is the setting for his creation and part of the artwork. In his favorite piece, *Nimbus D'Aspremont,* the architecture of the D'Aspremont-Lynden Castle in Rekem, Belgium, plays a significant role in the feel of the picture." Picture any sixth grader, from Brownsville or Flint, Michigan, reading that, without context, in the course of a three-day test.)

My scholars weren't the only ones having problems with these tests. Only 34.5 percent of city students in grades three to eight passed the Common Core math exams in 2014, and only 29.4 percent passed in reading and writing. There was much debate about whether the poor test results were the fault of the schools and students or of Pearson, the company accused of creating tests filled with ambiguous questions and inappropriate material. (Pearson was not hired to continue developing the New York State tests, so a whole new company with a whole new culture—and doubtless new books to sell us—would be creating the next year's tests.)

What began to weigh heavy on me was that at the same time I was struggling to get my scholars and their families to believe in themselves, I was part of an educational system that, despite its best intentions, only reinforced their failures. I was torn between focusing my time and energy on my numbers, the mandate from above, and following my instinct about the cultural, behavioral, and emotional things that need to be addressed with children, particularly those in middle school.

When you had low numbers, you were identified as a "focus" school. The terms used to be different: *turnaround schools, schools under reconstruction,* and others—there have been so many names over the years for schools where the test scores come in below proficient. All the families in any school identified as a focus school got a letter stating that their children's school was failing and that as parents they had the right—as part of the No Child Left Behind Act—to take them out of the school. Then the letter listed a number of other school options and announced an informational meeting at which they could learn about them.

The only reason I knew any of this was that a parent of one of my scholars approached me to say, "You know, Ms. Lopez, we got a card that said to transfer my son out. I ain't transferring him out."

"What?"

I was never notified by the Department of Education that these letters were going out. There is never a formal meeting to explain the implications of being a focus school or guidance on the process of being selected. I couldn't even figure out *who* on a state or city level sent the letters (and who I could complain to). That was the most disheartening part of the whole process, that there was no contact person or department in charge. For me, a principal leading a school, it was the ultimate lack of control over the situation.

Some may argue that if you have a good relationship with your parents, that's all that matters—in that when they trust that you have the best interest of their children at heart and actually see proof of learning, nothing the DOE says to the contrary will convince them otherwise. Only one parent at Mott Hall decided she was going to apply to send her child to another school. Still, the whole process undermined our credibility. For sure it made hiring harder. I sent out a letter to each of our parents putting the letter from the Department of Education or the state or whomever into context. (Just as I told Mr. Principal, we started out with kids who had some of the lowest scores in a poorly performing district. Improvement was improvement even if it was still considered below proficient.) I also made "Focus" one of Mott Hall's mottoes and put it on a T-shirt in an effort to bring the word back to its original, positive meaning.

Mott Hall Bridges didn't have the numbers, but I knew that the scholars loved their school because they told me in the hallways and wrote me letters or texts when they left—and their parents reiterated that sentiment. They loved it because their teachers believed in them, they were given choices, and their principal really cared about them. I have seen the limits of good numbers. In my brief experience in a charter network during my New Leaders residency, I saw the methods they used to get their test scores up, prizing that goal above all other types of work. I often wondered what those children would say if asked how they felt about their school. It was then that I decided I had larger goals for my scholars.

But, as I said, we're not measured on our culture; we're measured on the numbers. So if the kids don't show that they've improved on their numbers, it doesn't matter how much they love us. It doesn't matter how much they love their space. At the end of the day, someone is going to remind us that we're not good enough. That's the reason why schools close. It's not based on the social and emotional support that gets our kids to become resilient; it's about how much closer you are to closing an achievement gap defined by policy makers who have never stepped foot in Brooklyn, let alone Brownsville.

The data from the tests were a reminder that whatever I was doing at Mott Hall, it wasn't good enough. Instead of understanding low test scores through the lens of a broken system, they were used as tools of blame. No one ever sat leaders like me down to ask us what went wrong and how the process could be improved. The response was more warning e-mails, nervous phone calls, and questions about whose head needed to roll. No matter how much I tried to preempt mistakes, I was always reminded of the things that I didn't do.

Second-guessing is an occupational hazard since, as a

principal, there is no one to tell me right from wrong. The education system is set up so that we principals are all in our own buildings, doing our own thing (mainly trying to survive). That kind of autonomy might seem liberating, but when things aren't going right, you are the only person who is left to blame. Even harder is the fact that everyone needs a sounding board. I am the one who provides my teachers with professional development, connects them to mentors, and identifies networks in which they can share best practices. But if we principals want any of that, we must create it for ourselves.

Although I loved the opportunity to turn my vision for Mott Hall into a reality, being a principal could be an incredibly lonely job. In order to gain respect, you have to have boundaries with your subordinates. I've always made it clear to my team that I am not here to be their friend. I am here to educate children, make my staff better teachers, and transform a community. Achieving those goals requires me to focus entirely on my work, which means personal relationships are secondary. Ms. Achu is one of my closest friends—we celebrate birthdays together, have gone on vacations together, and share emotions—but when it comes to work, she is my subordinate. Outside we call each other by our first names, but in this building she is Ms. Achu, and I'm Ms. Lopez.

The huge amount of time a good principal spends at work only increases her sense of isolation. I try to reach out to friends, but it's hard for even those who know me the best to understand the demands of my profession. I can't count the number of people who have said to me, "You can't do everything. You need to quit that job." I know the sacrifices I make to do a job that has great meaning and at which I know I excel are unhealthy. I'm prone to mood swings (unfortunately often veering into the extremely irritated zone), and these affect my personal relationships as well.

It's important to commiserate with others who know what you are going through, which is why I missed the network that was a significant part of the New Leaders program. One particular mentor who stood out for me was Kinnari Patel-Smyth, the principal of the charter school I worked at during my residency. I enjoyed sharing moments of vulnerability with her, a leader who wasn't afraid to reveal times of being overwhelmed or struggling to find balance. Recently married, she wondered how she was going to navigate a family with the long hours her job demanded. "How do you do it with your daughter?" she asked me.

"I have my mom," I said. "I could not do this if it wasn't for her." It was so simple, but so true, and needed to be said.

That kind of give-and-take extended into all areas of our working relationship and made her a good mentor for me. She understood the demands of the organization, and just watching her deal with it all was a lesson. She had to manage so many personalities, including mine. Her confident leadership allowed me to thrive so that I could crystallize my own vision. Whereas she was extreme on the academic side, I'm extreme about social and emotional development. But she was never threatened when I pointed out concerns, such as what I noticed with boys like Jacob being punished for behavior whose root causes weren't examined. Instead, she used my input to help her think about her school from a different perspective.

In Mott Hall, however, I was in my own head virtually all the time. There wasn't even a network or a blueprint for me to follow. I built the structure as we went along. It was trial and error, except that I couldn't afford the error part. I had to be successful, because the stakes for my scholars were too high for me to fail them.

As much as I wanted to empower these young people and encourage them to be great and significant, the reality was that enormous and long-standing factors in the community often outweigh the power of my words. Brownsville is a place where racism and economic isolation have disenfranchised whole generations.

I know where I work; I know the statistics. According to the 2010 census data, the median household income in Brownsville is $28,838. But a 2012 study reported more than 55 percent of Brownsville residents received some type of income support. According to data released by New

York City in 2015, over one-quarter of adults living in Brownsville have not completed high school. Every year, graduation at Mott Hall is a big production, because many scholars—like Vincent—are the first in their families to graduate *from middle school*. We're trying to break odds. But how do you convince a community they can succeed when far and few have actually done that because of the lack of opportunity? How can you convince scholars they can succeed when they keep getting 1s on their state exams? You can't, because their takeaway is "*I'm* a 1."

The effect of all this on me was that I no longer slept. In order to turn off my brain, I had to take melatonin every night. Otherwise I was lucky to get three hours of sleep, after which I would be cranky and have to drink coffee all day. I never had trouble sleeping or drank coffee before I became a principal. I don't know if it was all the caffeine, the stress, or some combination of both, but I developed eosinophilic esophagitis: that's a chronic immune disease where my white blood cells attack my esophagus so that it feels like my insides are burning and shrinking. I started out with Tums and Rolaids before moving on to Mylanta. Then I segued to Prilosec, Nexium, and Protonix, until none of that worked and my doctor prescribed me an inhaled steroid.

As 2014 rolled to a close, I worried that I was slowly destroying myself for something that wasn't even working. Through images in the media, test scores, and what adults in their lives said to them, my scholars were *constantly reminded of failure.* If people wanted to charge the children of Mott Hall, Brownsville, and all underserved communities across this nation with apathy, well, I would say in reply that they've learned what they've been taught. When I told my scholars, which I did all the time, that they were smart, they believed it because they trusted me. But they also said, "Why is nobody else telling us that, Ms. Lopez?"

The kids never felt like they were winning, and I started to feel like I couldn't win either. I doubted whether anything I did made a difference and whether I mattered. I kept it to myself—cried in my office alone or stared at the ceiling at 3:00 A.M.—but I was broken.

CHAPTER EIGHT

PRAISE FOR HUMANS

I t was January 17, 2015—a Saturday—and my assistant principal, Mrs. K. Cadogan, and I were working late.

I always appreciated having Mrs. Cadogan around. Ever since joining the school that fall, she had been someone I could sit with and go through my thought process on everything from the execution of protocol to the ordering of supplies. Because I was so used to doing things on my own, it wasn't easy for me to say what I needed. But I trusted her, which is not always the case with principals and their vice-principals, whom principals often treat as fillers, warm bodies to stand in for them when they can't be there. Mrs. Cadogan and I had the same beliefs and vision.

Another recent and unexpected addition to the Mott Hall Bridges team was Ms. DeCoteau, my coteacher during my first job in education at McKinney and my inspiration for so much. Not long after I left the Fort Greene middle school, Ms. DeCoteau followed suit. As she described it, her reason for leaving was that she was fed up with "a lot of the new rules and conditions placed on teachers that had nothing to do with teaching," such as the Department of Education's hands-off policy, which meant teachers couldn't touch students for any reason, even to break up fights. So after fifteen years as a teacher, Ms. DeCoteau left teaching and returned to the Caribbean, where she was born and raised.

Four years later, though, in January 2015, she was back in Brooklyn and paid me a surprise visit at Mott Hall. Ms. Manning, my staff developer, had orchestrated the meeting. Ms. DeCoteau and I both broke down because we hadn't seen each other in so long. When I found out she wasn't teaching, I immediately asked if she could help me out by assisting one of my teachers. She said yes, because she knew that we shared the same philosophy that a teacher should meet the child where the child is at. However, she made it clear she wasn't at all sure about returning to teaching.

Ms. DeCoteau, who started as a substitute a week later, wound up staying at Mott Hall, where she found a home filled with like-minded individuals willing to support one another in supporting the children. The support she needed revolved around learning the language of the Common Core. As soon as she came back, I identified this as an area where she needed extra help, but I didn't want her to get bogged down by it; good teaching is good teaching no matter what you call it. When you hear the widespread complaint that Common Core kills great teaching, it is because people are focusing too much on terminology instead of just getting down to doing it.

Since before we were teachers together at McKinney, Ms. DeCoteau had been asking the good, higher-level questions that get scholars to reflect, state claims, and provide evidence for their claims (all elements of the Common Core). When I decided to link her with a few other teachers so she could align her teaching practice with the Common Core language, it was more about reassuring Ms. DeCoteau that she was already doing what was being asked. However, she was eager to work with the other teachers. "You know how we do, Lopez," she said. "We'll get this." And she did.

But none of that mattered as Mrs. Cadogan and I prepared for the superintendent and all the other principals in our district to do a walk-through of Mott Hall the following week. They would observe classrooms and offer feedback. I love my school, and I love to share what we are doing here in innovative programming, support for our kids, and professional development. I wanted this tour to show us at our best. But as I went through the halls and classrooms on Saturday, I saw opportunities for criticism everywhere. By the time we entered a classroom where the bulletin board still had work up from two months earlier, I was at the end of my rope. How had I let this happen?

Of course, I knew how this had happened. It had been a hard year—not unlike our first—because the sixth graders who came in were the lowest-performing scholars we'd ever had. They struggled academically, and because of that they struggled socially. My staff was exhausted; I was exhausted. I had reached out to my superintendent right before Christmas to say that I was stretched beyond my capacity. My superintendent said I was being too hard on myself, but I felt like I was dropping the ball.

While I was pulling down the November classwork from the bulletin board, the school custodian stuck his head in. "Ms. Lopez, we've got to go," he said. They had to lock up the building. I was going to have to return on Sunday because Monday was Martin Luther King, Jr., Day and I was hosting one of my youth leadership conferences on the holiday.

I was angry when I arrived home, angry about everything—the bulletin board, the race against time, the system. I had recently hired a data specialist to look at our stats, and he proved to me what I basically already knew: a large percentage of my scholars came into Mott Hall scoring in the bottom third of all New York City public school students. It is in the fourth grade that the Department of Education identifies this group based on state exam scores, tracking these students until the end of high school. Society is always hand-wringing over these boys—asking, What can we do?—and yet I don't get any extra money to raise my scholars in the bottom third. The system would rather plan for failure than strategize toward success.

I was most angry, however, with myself. Long before that day, I had worried that I was becoming a detriment to Mott Hall. My heart was in the right place, but I wondered if my relentless drive to do what I felt we were supposed to wasn't actually holding others back. You know, the classic control freak issues: "If she doesn't like it, she's going to do it herself. If I don't come in, she's going to teach." My mentality was always that if you don't do it, I'm going to, because it's my school.

But now I was at my breaking point. Whenever I got home and either my mother or my daughter needed something from me, I had no patience for them. "Everybody wants something of me. You all don't understand what I have to go through at work. So I don't need to come home and deal with the stress of your demands." Even if I didn't say those exact words, I made them clear enough. I also began to share fatalistic thoughts with thirteen-year-old Cenné about how she needed to be independent because my mother was getting on in years and my own health was a mess. "If something happens to me, you don't have anyone else," I told her.

I had been spiraling for a while, but when I returned home from the long day trying to get Mott Hall ready for the review, I was totally defeated. I flopped down on the couch and started to cry.

"What? What's wrong?" my mother asked.

"I don't want to do this anymore. I'm so tired."

"What do you mean?"

"Mommy, I can't. I'm tired of taking pills. I'm tired of running this rat race. I'm tired of my daughter feeling like she's not good enough because I'm never home. I'm writing my letter of resignation."

"No. You need to pray about your situation."

"I don't feel like it."

"God put you in that position because he knows what you can take. So you can't allow yourself this one moment."

"I'll pray tomorrow."

I knew that this "one moment" was the culmination of so many moments.

"Okay. I'm going to pray for you," my mother declared.

The next day I did decide to go to church, figuring at least the music would do me some good, but Cenné asked if I could drop her off at Mott Hall so she could travel with the boys' basketball team to watch their game at a school in Sheepshead Bay. I agreed, since it was on my way to church and it was pouring outside, but when I arrived at school there were all these kids standing out in this torrential rainstorm. When I asked what was going on, Mr. McLeod replied that they didn't have enough cars to take all the boys to the game.

"Ms. Lopez, can we get into your car?" the boys asked.

"I'm going to church. I've got to pray."

"Please, Ms. Lopez, please?"

I'm not kidding, I was trying to roll up the windows on these boys begging me. But then Cenné gave me a look like, "Mommy, really?"

"Fine. Get in the car," I said, when all I wanted was my little Jesus music.

To top it off, we lost the game.

"You all need to step up," I snapped at the boys on the way home. "You're acting selfish. Teams consist of people working together. You have to own it!"

The next day was the youth summit at Mott Hall in honor of MLK day. It was just Monday, and already I was tired. As I went in and out of classrooms to see if people needed anything I noted that out of the two hundred kids and adults who showed up, only two children were from Mott Hall. In that moment, I really wanted to give up.

There was no time for reflection, though. When the summit was over that afternoon, my day was just beginning. I picked up Cenné to go to my cousin's fashion trade show in Manhattan, after which we were headed to see *Mamma Mia!* on Broadway. We took our seats a few minutes before the 8:00 P.M. curtain time, and as the lights in the theater dimmed, I quickly looked at my phone. That's when I saw a text from a teacher asking, "Did you see this?"

It was a snapshot of a picture on the Internet of one of my scholars, Vidal. He was standing on a street corner in Brownsville with a black hoodie up over his head.

"Turn off all phones," an usher said to me.

I was more concerned about what had happened to Vidal. After Trayvon Martin was shot dead in Florida, no one could ever look at a sweatshirt as simple apparel again. At least not for a black boy. But when Cenné said, "Mommy!" I shut the phone down.

For an entire hour, I sat with *Mamma Mia!* going on right in front of me but didn't see any of it because my mind was on Vidal, what he might have said, or what he might have done. Vidal, an eighth grader at Mott Hall, was a loving young man. Close to his mother, who'd immigrated from St. Lucia and was raising him and his brothers on her own, Vidal helped her out by doing the laundry, watching his brothers, and cleaning. He wasn't the kind of kid who ran in the streets.

As soon as it was intermission, I turned my phone back on, and the first text I saw was from one of my former scholars, Terrance, who wrote, "You're an inspiration."

Where did that come from? What did I do?

I went on the Web site with Vidal's picture; it was a

blog called *Humans of New York*. And there, under a shot of Vidal, was a short interview with him:

> *Who's influenced you the most in your life?*
> My principal, Ms. Lopez.
> *How has she influenced you?*
> When we get in trouble, she doesn't suspend us. She calls us to her office and explains to us how society was built down around us. And she tells us that each time somebody fails out of school, a new jail cell gets built. And one time she made every student stand up, one at a time, and she told each one of us that we matter.

Wow. That was beautiful. Now I was inspired. I started scrolling through comments, which were so moving that by the time we left the theater and got back in the car, I was crying. The outpouring from strangers for this blog post was overwhelming. On Facebook, there were 15,000 likes and 3,000 comments. That, however, was just the start. By the time I got home, there were something like 300,000 likes.

I showed it to my mom, who said, "Who's Ms. Lopez? Are you Ms. Lopez?"

"Yeah, Ma. Just read the comments."

My mother sat there for hours, trying to read every

single comment. "This is so beautiful," she said. "And you thought you didn't matter."

She read some of the comments out loud:

> U have made so many people proud and have brought good tidings to your school. God bless u.
>
> All because one woman was kind to and believed in one boy. ♥
>
> His was absolutely one of my most favorite HONY photographs. It was invigorating to read about a shift in the system . . . ; that along with my fellow teachers at my campus, there are others in high-risk areas who do not simply follow the "traditional" consequence model of chastising the student, and simply throwing the book at them without allowing for reflection.
>
> I don't get choked up often, but when I do, it's for inspiring people like this young man and Ms. Lopez.

Those were from strangers on Facebook (where Vidal's post eventually logged more than 1 million likes, 24,000 comments, and 145,000 shares), but friends, colleagues, and students past and present were blasting my phone with texts. I think the last one came in at 4:00 A.M. One of my teachers texted, "Here I am, thinking to myself I should call out sick, and wondering whether or not I should even do this work anymore. And I see this *Humans of New York* piece about you. And I thought to myself, 'If she can impact that many lives, then who am I to complain?' I'll see you in the morning."

"I'll see you in the morning," I texted back.

"You're up, really?"

"Yeah, I'm up."

But perhaps the most important text came from Brandon Stanton, the man behind *Humans of New York* and the photographer who had taken the picture of Vidal. Brandon's story was that after he lost his job as a bond trader in Chicago, he decided to move to New York to take portraits of ordinary people. He was relentless in his approach, shooting for six to eight hours a day and taking fewer than ten days off during his first three years of the project. His hard work paid off in 12.8 million followers on Facebook, 2.5 million on Instagram, and 1 million on Tumblr (and eventually a *New York Times* best-selling book). I liked him before we even met.

After Vidal's post garnered millions of views, Brandon came to visit Mott Hall and asked me why Vidal pointed out that I take time with each kid. "Sometimes our kids act up because we don't listen to them, and they just don't know how to explain themselves," I said. "Everyone has a story, and it's very powerful."

"Do you know my blog?" he asked.

The truth was I *didn't* know his blog all that well—
other than how it had turned my life upside down in the
last few days. But Brandon was just saying that because
Humans of New York is about the very same thing: telling
people's stories.

I took him to a meeting with my staff, where he listened to their stories about why they got into education
and what it's like being a teacher at Mott Hall Bridges. He
found a few compelling enough to put them up on his Web
site. For instance, Ms. Kinsale said:

> I can teach a lot of things. But it's so hard to
> teach effort. It's so hard to teach want. And
> there are certain days when it seems like the
> scholars don't care, and you feel like no matter
> how hard you try, nothing is getting through,
> and the negative thoughts get louder and louder,
> and it's easy to feel worthless. And today was
> one of those days. Normally I'm always the one
> with a smile on my face, cheering everybody up.
> But today was one of those days.

Or Ms. O:

> I came from a very poor family. My father
> was a small farmer in Nigeria. And even though
> he had no education, he always taught me that

education was the most important thing. He told me: "When you have no education, it's like being in a small room with many people. There is little opportunity available to you, and many people are competing with you. But as you educate yourself, the room grows. You have more opportunities, and less people competing with you." I always remembered that. My mother died when I was twelve. I started working as a maid when I turned thirteen. I made five cents a day, which I saved for school. There was no free education in Nigeria. When I ran out of money, I'd stop going to school and go back to work. Stop, work, go back to school. Stop, work, go back to school. And all along my father would say, "You aren't done yet. This is not your last bus stop. One day you will have so much education that you will teach in America."

After that Brandon couldn't stay away from Mott Hall. He kept returning to take more pictures and hear more stories, like this one from Mott Hall's student government president, Adrian:

I want to make it out of the hood. I don't have to go that far. But if I can just live an inch out-

side, then I'll feel safe and know that I'm
straight.

Brandon kept the story going and going for us, because
he saw that the kids loved it at their school, which honored
people's voices. Less than two weeks after he posted the
picture of Vidal, he asked what he could do to help us. He
had done fund-raisers for a few of his other subjects—
including raising almost $80,000 toward the fees for a
New York family to adopt a boy from Ethiopia and $30,000
for a little boy he found selling stuff in Washington Square
Park for the chance to ride a horse. (All the extra money,
after the cost for the boy and his family to go to a dude
ranch for a week, went to an organization that gives riding
lessons to children with disabilities.)

"What would you like to do for your kids if you could
do anything?" he asked.

Without even needing to think about it, I said, "I want
to take them to Harvard."

With its history of Ivy League privilege, Harvard University might have seemed like a provocative or naive
choice of college for my scholars to visit, but it came from
my gut.

I had visited Harvard while I was in the New Leaders
program. It wasn't part of the plan, but we were at an
IHOP in Cambridge after a conference when Geo, one of

my fellow New Leaders and a good friend, suggested we visit the campus.

"I don't know, Geo," I said.

"We're already here," he replied, like it was no big deal.

But it was a big deal to me. I thought the Ivy League institution was a white-male-dominated, pretentious college, where everyone was rich. I was afraid of being in a space in which it would be immediately clear I didn't belong. I anticipated feeling like I had no worth, and who wants that?

When we walked around, however, I was surprised to discover that nobody asked me for my ID or looked at me because I'm a person of color. Like Vassar, Harvard is a beautiful school that I enjoyed touring. The whole experience caused me to reevaluate my assumptions—not only about Harvard but also about myself.

Where did I get the idea that I wasn't good enough for the Ivy League? No teacher or principal, or one of my parents ever said that I'd be insane to apply to Harvard. No one ever mentioned the word *Harvard*. The omission was the problem.

When I had created Mott Hall, I'd vowed that my kids were going to know that they could go anywhere. So when Brandon asked me what I wanted, I thought, *All right. You're thinking we can raise some money. I'm going to go for the gusto; we're going to Harvard.*

"How much would that cost?" Brandon asked without missing a beat.

"Maybe thirty thousand dollars if we take the whole school."

"Let's do it for three years."

Who was I to say no? With Brandon as our guide, we planned a crowd-funding campaign to raise $100,000 for three years of trips to take Mott Hall scholars to Harvard.

On January 22, the day the fund-raiser went up online, Brandon came to Mott Hall and told me, "The response to Mott Hall has been really great. They're in love with your story and your school. I'm letting you know, hold on to your seat."

"Okay, Brandon," I said. I mean, I believed in dreams, but there is a limit.

About forty-five minutes after the campaign went up, I was coming out of the bathroom when one of my teachers said, "Ms. Lopez, we made it!"

"Made what?"

"The hundred thousand dollars!"

"The hundred thousand dollars on what?"

"For the fund-raiser?"

"In forty-five minutes?"

"Yeah."

My former students from P.S. 73, Keandra and Eve, both in college by then, had happened to come to Mott Hall that day, so they were there when we made the first

$100,000. "The only reason why we're in college is because Ms. Lopez took us to Vassar," they told Brandon and my school superintendent, who was also in the building. "That was not something we even thought about. We went because she showed us what the possibilities were."

What happened over the next several hours (by 5:00 P.M., the fund-raiser had hit $300,000, enough to take scholars to Harvard for ten years) and the next several days were a whirlwind the likes of which not even I could have imagined.

For the first time, Brownsville, Brooklyn, made international and national headlines with a positive story. Many newspapers, networks, and Web sites sent reporters to talk to Vidal, Brandon, and me. Mott Hall's story was covered in the *New York Times,* the New York *Daily News, Essence,* on CNN, PBS—and picked up by outlets across the country and around the globe, including the BBC, the *Washington Post,* and the *San Francisco Chronicle.*

People just fell in love with our story, which came to the attention of Ellen DeGeneres, who invited us to appear on her popular daytime TV show. Vidal, Brandon, and I flew out to L.A. on February 2 and headed straight to the studio to tape the segment.

The producer in charge of prepping guests worried I wasn't "excited" enough and tried to script us, but he had the wrong person. I'm nothing if not authentic and will be excited when it's time to get excited.

"She's the principal," Brandon said with a laugh.

The producer didn't need to worry; there wasn't a dry eye in the house when Ellen announced that Target was providing Mott Hall Bridges and other schools in Browns-ville with $100,000 worth of iPads and other electronics.

We had to fly home immediately because on February 4 we taped a segment for *Good Morning America* at Mott Hall. *GMA* host Robin Roberts, whose mother was spurred to go to college by one of her elementary school teachers, had a personal connection to our story.

"Ms. Schnegg is a legend in our family, because she made sure my mother knew that she was expected to go to college," Robin Roberts told Brandon for his blog. "She sat down and helped my mother apply for a hundred-dollar scholarship, and my mother used that scholarship to go to Howard University. And that one act rippled down through several generations. Because of that, my mother met my father. And they raised four children who went to college. And because of Ms. Schnegg, I'm where I am to-day. So I look at the story of Ms. Lopez and this school, and I think of Ms. Schnegg, and I think of how much my mother would have loved this story." *Good Morning Amer-ica, Ellen,* and the money that continued to flow into our crowd-funding campaign would have been completely overwhelming if we had been able to stop to think about it. But the same day that we taped our *GMA* segment, we found out we were going to meet the president of the United States.

Brandon, the point of contact, hadn't known we were invited to the White House until twenty-four hours before. Of course, once everything started to blow up, I thought the greatest thing would be for us to meet Barack Obama. That's why, when we were in L.A. to tape *Ellen,* we made a quick detour to Macy's to buy a suit for Vidal. Even our shopping experience seemed to indicate a trip to the Oval Office was in the stars, because when we walked in the door, the suit was right there. Vidal tried it on and it was perfect. We got the tie, stood in line, and in less than twenty minutes we were back in the car. Looking at Brandon, I said, "Something *has* to happen from here."

As soon as Brandon got the news that this *was* happening—the next day, February 5—we had to tell Vidal and his mom the news so they could get ready.

"So listen. We're going to see the president," Brandon said to her.

"You are kidding, right?" she said, before she began to laugh giddily.

"The president of the United States wants to speak to *us*?" Vidal said.

"We need you to get dressed and get your bags together," he said.

"By when?"

"Today. Now! We've got to be there tomorrow."

"Are you all serious?"

"Yes! But y'all need to hurry up."

We jumped into a ride—Brandon had gotten us an extended SUV—and stopped at my house so I could get some clothes. As soon as I walked in the door and saw my mother's face, I knew something was wrong.

"Your grandmother. I don't think she's going to make it," my mother said about my ninety-seven-year-old *abuela,* who lived in Guatemala. After hearing that news, the last thing I felt like doing was going to D.C., but both of us knew I had to. When I got back down to the car, I told Brandon to move over. I was driving, because that's my therapy. He asked if I was okay, and I explained that my grandmother was dying.

"Do you need time?" he asked.

"Nope. I just need to drive," I said.

The next morning was bitterly cold as we walked the three blocks from our hotel to the White House, where we had to wait in line. There was a lot of press there—not for Mott Hall but for a statement the president was making about ISIS—and we had to wait for them to go before checking in. I brought an "I Matter" T-shirt with me, because the president just had to have one. Security asked me who the T-shirt was for and I explained, the president. So then I had to go through all these levels of security to clear the item. I was like, "It's a T-shirt." Finally, after it passed the last level, a special assistant, who came to take us to see Mr. Obama, said I had to leave the T-shirt because he couldn't accept gifts. They could have told me that before all the security checks! It didn't matter; nothing could ruin this moment.

We were led to an eerily quiet back area, where we waited until another staffer told us we had to stand in front of a door. When the president was ready for us, the person explained, he would open it.

We must have been waiting for about four minutes, but it felt like four hundred. Just standing there was pure torture. Out of sheer nerves, I took out my phone, thinking, *Let me see what's going on in the world; who do I need to e-mail or anything like that?* But as soon as I went for my phone, the door opened onto this bright, shining light. It was *him*.

"Hey, how's it going?" the president said.

Vidal responded by fainting into Brandon's arms. "Vidal!" I said. He quickly pulled himself together, and we went into a beautifully sunlit Oval Office.

Despite the magnitude of the occasion and my respect for the company, my focus remained on Vidal. My work wasn't to be in awe of Mr. Obama but to be proud that I had prepared my scholar for this moment. As Vidal asked the president who inspired him, I noted the poise of this young man. Wearing a purple tie (a purple tie!) and holding his hands in the same measured way the president did, Vidal knew he could be in this space and that he belonged.

Brandon, Vidal, and I had an opportunity to ask Mr. Obama one question each. When it came to my turn, only one thing was in my head. "When was a time you felt broken?" I asked.

I think the reason I asked him that was because, when I looked at the president, I felt every sacrifice he may have made as a leader—the times he wasn't with his children because he had a job to do or the times people hurled unfair accusations at him that he had no choice but to weather. I could see how much grayer his hair had become since he took office. In answer to my question, he told us about when he first ran for Congress, in 1999–2000. "I just got whooped," he said. "There was a stretch of time when I was forty, when I had invested a lot of time in something, and I wasn't sure whether I'd taken the right path. I think we all go through those stretches. You know, usually life's not a straight line."

Sitting face-to-face with President Obama, I looked at him as a leader who believed his work was to make a change. By being the first person of color to break an important barrier by holding the highest office in the land, he showed an entire community that we have value in the American system. He got here, and yet, some don't respect him. He got here, and yet, whatever he does still doesn't seem like it's good enough. I could relate to Mr. Obama in that I knew what it was to have a vision and struggle every day to achieve it.

That's why—in addition to affording my scholars opportunities—the money Brandon helped Mott Hall raise meant so much to me. It was like an answer to my feelings of being alone and broken, that no one was listening.

In the fourteen days we kept the crowd-funding site up, we raised $1,418,334 from 51,466 people around the world. With those kinds of numbers, I couldn't deny what I was doing had an impact. People did care.

Although the bulk of that money was going to be put toward a summer program to continue the work we do the rest of the year to build self-esteem and academic progress ("summer slide" in Brownsville is clearly a lot more detrimental than forgetting what you learned in math class), as well as into a scholarship fund, we still had our original plan to go to Harvard. There was just one little problem: I had never spoken to anyone at Harvard about the plan.

"After going on *Ellen* and telling the president of the United States that we are going to Harvard, do you think maybe we should call them and have a meeting?" I asked Ms. Achu.

We got in contact with Harvard administrators, who were so enthusiastic about our visit that they created a planning committee for it. In the weeks leading up to the trip, the committee came to Mott Hall to speak to my staff.

Each teacher received a bag that contained a Harvard pennant and a book with all the materials they would need for the trip, which the committee walked us through. They also brought bins filled with about two hundred crimson-covered notebooks embossed with Harvard's name in gold for the scholars to use for journaling.

It was exciting for everyone at the school, because Harvard's investment of money, time, and thought was evident to all. In our planning of the trip, the impact of the whole story of our school finally hit the rest of the scholars. Up until then I don't know that they understood the magnitude of what was happening. They knew that there was a lot of press coming to Mott Hall and money being raised, but they didn't connect to it, because it all seemed tied to Vidal. When we went to meet the president, it was Vidal sitting there. When we went to appear on *Ellen,* it was Vidal. While some of them and their parents were proud, they didn't really feel like this meant *they* were important.

The really big moment came when the entire school—sixth, seventh, and eighth grades—loaded onto the five buses we'd chartered to go to Harvard. Finally they could see this money was for them and they were getting to experience something special. The buses were scheduled to leave Brownsville at 5:30 A.M., but kids arrived with their parents as early as 4:45. Waiting as the sun rose were scholars with chronic attendance issues, the ones who never show up on time, ever, and parents we hadn't seen in over a year. There was no doubt in any of the parents' minds that "my kid" was getting on that bus.

Not every kid, however, got to go to Harvard. Out of the school's about eighty scholars, fourteen weren't allowed on the trip. The kids we did not take were those who had demonstrated such a profound lack of respect for adults or authority in the building that they didn't earn the opportunity.

The one scholar I insisted go on the trip—just as I had done with Kyle and Vassar back at P.S. 73—was Antonne, the boy who had showed a lot of defiance after watching his father get shot on a playground. I took so much heat for that kid, both to my face and behind my back. Ironically, Mr. Principal didn't think Antonne had worked hard enough to go to Harvard. If he could go, the teacher argued, why couldn't Kimberly, who I said had to stay back because of her behavior. My answer was that Antonne inflicted pain on himself by not doing his work, but he didn't try to hurt other people. She might be compliant in class, but outside, Kimberly was constantly beating up on and bullying girls. I put my energy into her in a different way—namely the amount of time I spent with the NYPD and mentors to support her.

I treated Antonne the way I did because if I hadn't, I would have lost him a long time ago. So my staff, who felt like he didn't suffer the consequences of his attitude, could be mad at me. What more could he suffer than watching his father get shot in a place where he was playing? How I dealt with him was not a cop-out. I wanted him not to be afraid to talk to the adults around him, to learn that we were there for him, and, most of all, to graduate. So, yeah, Antonne went to Harvard.

From the minute we got off the bus in Cambridge, everything was well planned by the university. Our first stop was the Harvard Art Museums' Calderwood Courtyard, where we were greeted by the president of the university, Drew Gilpin Faust. The first woman to lead Harvard, she talked about inviting her sixth-grade geography teacher to her presidential inauguration. "I remembered what a hard grader he was and how difficult he had made life for me in the sixth grade. But these many years later we were reconciled over how much I'd learned then, and how much it had mattered to me for so very long," she said. "One day you will be seeing perhaps your teachers standing in front of you celebrating your achievements as you move into life and build on what they're teaching you now. They are inspiring, I know, and that inspiration, I can tell you, lasts throughout your lifetime."

When I spoke after Dr. Faust, I drove home that what we as educators had been preparing our students for was their birthright, but they still had to want it. "This is your right, and this is an option for you," I said. "The only thing that will stop you from getting to this space is yourselves." If these scholars could wake up and be at a school at 4:45 A.M. to go to Harvard, we knew they could be at school on time every day. We were finally winning.

The day was filled with rich discussion. Harvard had organized a panel discussion with four university students, who spoke about coming from single-family homes or families that didn't have enough money to send them to college. One young man explained how it was cheaper for him to go to Harvard, which offered him a full scholarship, than to go to the University of Texas in his home state, where he would have had a combination of scholarships and loans. Another student talked about being raised by a single mom, who as a teacher didn't have the money to send him to Harvard but always taught him he would make it somewhere. "And here I am," he said.

While not all the students looked like my scholars— there were two white people, one Spanish woman, and a biracial man—they offered descriptions of circumstances not far from what the kids at Mott Hall experienced. In less than an hour, those four students shattered the stereotypes that all Harvard students are white people from wealthy, two-parent households. If education is exposure, which I believe it is, a lot of learning got done that day.

Then came the best part, the experiential learning, a taste of what it was like to actually go to college. After the organizing committee had met with us back at Mott Hall, they'd sent out an e-mail to Harvard professors seeking volunteers to teach versions of their classes tailored to middle school kids. The result was a soft robotics demonstration at the Harvard Biodesign Lab, a look at zebrafish at the Harvard Museum of Natural History, a class on hip-hop, and more. One of my eighth graders, Melody, told the *Harvard Gazette* that she had been so excited to visit the Hiphop Archive & Research Institute, she couldn't sleep the night before. "I woke up every hour checking the time," she said.

The admiration wasn't just one way. At the ends of the classes, a lot of the professors and the Harvard students said the scholars had demonstrated a high level of intellect. They'd asked great questions and had an impressive knowledge base. The professor who offered a class on Chinese art was amazed at how the kids could have a conversation about why an artist used a particular medium and what that reflected about the culture of the time. I explained that my art teacher, Ms. Dorn, teaches fundamentals of art history while the students are doing their own art projects because she believes, "You need to know why you're making it." So it wasn't only the scholars being validated; their teachers, seeing their hard work through the eyes of other top educators, realized, *Yes, I am doing a good job*. The excitement lasted long after our trip ended. Certainly you could feel the energy in the kids for the entire bus ride home. Usually when we take students on college trips, it's in groups of ten or twelve. This experience of the entire Mott Hall Bridges Academy descending on Harvard was profoundly different, because we made an impact on the college. Even just visually, to have all those young scholars of color walking the quad was different and empowering. And Harvard students who had followed our story were coming up to our scholars like they were famous, encouraging them to keep going. So our visit to Harvard wasn't just a view into one of the premier learning institutions in the world but a whole community rallying behind our students.

On the bus ride home, the scholars couldn't wait to share what they had experienced with their parents. Because of traffic delays, our arrival time was pushed back, and as it got later and later, I anticipated complaints from the parents waiting in front of the school. But when we got off that bus, not one person in the crowd waiting grumbled. It was just the opposite. They were jubilant at the sight of their children descending from the bus with their Harvard notebooks.

Amid all the blessings, tears, smiles, and hugs, I spotted Antonne's mom—and his grandmother. They were both there to see that boy get off that bus. "Thank you, Ms. Lopez," his mom said. "For always looking out for Antonne."

In that moment I thought, *This is why I do what I do.*

CHAPTER NINE

NEVER GIVE UP

"Those your bros?" Antonne asked Vidal, who didn't respond.

"Yes or no," I said. *"Yes or no."*

"I seen it with my own eyes," Antonne, in a rage, continued. "I haven't fought since seventh grade. I ain't holding back no more. I lost two bros to this. And I ain't holding back no more. Those not your bros. They ain't going to run back for you. They just saw on TV like everyone else."

Vidal, Antonne, Coach Randy, and I were sitting in the conference room in late May, almost two months after the Harvard trip, because Vidal was out in the streets. More specifically, he'd been spotted around the Seth Low Houses. Usually kids from the Brownsville Houses, like Antonne and Vidal, don't deal with the Seth Low Houses unless they're cool with other boys—meaning affiliated with a gang.

Antonne had alerted Coach Randy to the fact not because he was afraid but because he was mad. I wasn't sure what bothered him more, that Vidal was associating with people from a rival gang or that the symbol of Mott Hall's success was out on the streets at all.

Over the last month or so, Vidal had taken to hanging out in the school building until 9:00 P.M., but I had told him he couldn't do that because grown men played basketball there after hours and I was responsible for his safety when he was in the building. "So take yourself home," I said. "Do your work and be the big brother so your little brothers can follow behind you."

What I didn't know was that Vidal had been jumped twice the previous month. Instead of telling me what was going on, he engaged in a form of avoidance that so many kids in his situation do. To be told by me that he couldn't stay in school was just another rejection. So Vidal became focused on the need to hang around people who were going to accept and protect him. In general, that is why gangs are so prevalent in this neighborhood and others like it; kids are looking for spaces where people are going to accept them. Vidal, however, isn't a street kid.

"You think we don't know what you do when you leave here?" I said to Vidal. "You know I always find out."

It was tense around the conference room table. Antonne was jittery with anger, waiting for some kind of answer from Vidal, who kept his gaze firmly on the floor. Only Coach Randy had a kind of bemused look, the one that Coach Randy *always* has.

"I would rather you go to Van Dykes than Seth Low or Howard," I said. "You are going through sections where someone could take you out. Vidal, on the streets no one cares if you don't make it. If someone kills you, they will become famous."

"It's shocking, because you aren't a street dude," Coach Randy said.

"And it's nothing to be ashamed about," I said. "I'm not a street kid, but growing up, I knew how to survive and get out of trouble. I grew up in that time when they left bodies out with sheets on them for everyone to look at. My middle school was in Fort Greene, where they started the notorious Decepticons gang. Between crack wars and gun violence, I made it; you can make it. But if you keep this up, you are going to be dead. There are too many young black men dying. I didn't open up a school to fund funeral parlors or prisons."

"You should thank Antonne," Coach Randy said. "He didn't need to sit me down and tell me. Instead I could have found out about you wilding when you're being chased down Blake Ave."

"Everyone snitchin'," Antonne said. "I'm a hard head and I know that. You still have a chance. Before they get a chance to know you, turn your back. If you end up in jail, only your mom's going to be behind you."

This moment filled me with a mixture of pain and pride. Vidal was struggling, like all of us at Mott Hall—scholars, staff, and principal included—and that never gets any easier to witness. But at the same time, here was Antonne, who came to us as a sixth grader troubled because someone had tried to execute his father over the summer, fully owning the school creed of respect and citizenship. Perhaps Antonne had been emboldened to rise above the fray by a promotional video Harvard had created about the scholars' visit to the campus. In one section, a few of the children talk about what they want to do in the future, and one of them was Antonne. "Architecture and design," he said, with the red brick and Doric columns of Harvard Yard's Memorial Church as the backdrop. "I want to have my own architecture firm. I am going to stay in school, graduate, and go to college."

I was so happy to send that video out to the entire staff, most of whom didn't think Antonne should go on the trip at all, because in it he sounded like a kid from Brownsville with ideas. I took this moment to honor that.

"You went to Harvard and you are on the video," I said to Antonne. "You spoke into existence what you want for yourself. I know there are street gangs and street codes, but what you are learning here is to better your family.

Your sister is coming behind you. You can't tell her all the great things about Mott Hall if you end up just like everyone else. So do me this favor, sir, I need you to make it. All this time and energy will not be wasted. Do you understand?"

"Yes, Ms. Lopez," Antonne said.

"You two are in a good space with someone who really, really loves and believes in you. They want you to act like a savage beast on the street and kill yourselves or go to jail, because there is nothing like an intelligent man of color. *That's* dangerous.

"I have been given special honors, because of my work with you all. Barnard College gave me its Medal of Distinction, and I was up on that stage during BET's *Black Girls Rock!* getting an award along with Jada Pinkett Smith and Michelle Obama because of *you*. Do you know how special that is?"

"Thank you for this conversation," Coach Randy said, standing up. "I love the both of you. Remember, Antonne, how I chased you into the park until you stopped cursing about getting off the court. And, Vidal, understand you are a kid with a lot of opportunities in front of you. You're not a street kid. It's cool. Just know your lane."

I needed to rethink Vidal. I couldn't have him feeling rejected by his school. I would have him stay for an hour after school to do homework, then maybe find him a place to play basketball. I wasn't kidding that all this time and energy wouldn't be wasted. I also wanted them to become lifelong friends and a network for each other.

What I wanted for Vidal was what I want for all Mott Hall's children. As I told him, "Vidal, you have a golden ticket, but it comes with a lot of pressure. I get it. People think this place is perfect because of our story, but we have flaws. And a lot of them. Still, I am going to capitalize on every opportunity to give every scholar access to a world outside of Brownsville, and you will too. You need to start thinking of yourself as a leader and use your voice, because you have a story that goes beyond *Humans of New York*."

Making sure Vidal continues his story after he leaves Mott Hall is why when a prestigious parochial high school offered him a full scholarship, I insisted the admissions director, who reached out to me, come meet me so we could have a face-to-face talk about Vidal. Vidal's fame gave him access, but he would still need to be supported to succeed. And whatever high school he attended would have to understand that fully.

The Catholic school's guidance counselor and athletic director made the time to come to Mott Hall, which I greatly appreciated. I explained that I wanted them to make it very clear to Vidal that this scholarship came with expectations. "You can't just give him something or he'll think people are always going to be giving him things, without him needing to put in the hard work," I said. "And that is the surest path to failure."

When they returned to officially offer Vidal the scholarship, which included the cost of tuition and an orientation program, both the high school and Mott Hall had agreed to a partnership over this young man.

"We are going to give you a full scholarship to school, if you are willing to take it," the coach from Vidal's new school told him in my office. "You have to keep this scholarship. That means you have to work with me. We are going to take care of business. And it doesn't start in ninth grade. It starts now. So finish up as strong as you can. Work hard."

"Our job is to protect you as much as Ms. Lopez did," the guidance counselor said. "We want to continue doing what she did for you."

Vidal was literally speechless. In the movie version of his life, he would have jumped up, hugged the guidance counselor, and pumped the coach's hand in thanks. But this was real life, and Vidal could only sit there with a glazed expression. He wasn't rude; he was stunned. I could only imagine the mix of excitement, fear, confusion, pride, and who-knows-what other feelings inside of him as he faced this unknown path.

After a few moments of awkward silence, I said, "It's a lot." Then the coach gave Vidal a little package that he explained contained a letter with the school's expectations for the scholarship and their personal phone numbers. "We aren't just handing you something," he said. "But if you need anything, you come to us directly."

The parochial school made a commitment to put a whole support team in place for Vidal and keep communicating with Mott Hall about his progress. It still wasn't going to be easy for Vidal. But as Barack Obama had told him when he sat in the Oval Office, "You don't do things alone. Nobody does things alone. Everybody always needs support. A lot of people like to help. So you'll have a lot of people supporting you out there. You will just have to make sure that you seize those opportunities."

Anyone who has made it in this life—whether or not he or she is honest about it—had an advocate. I know I had many. Ms. Holmes, the school administrator who allowed me to stay late and help out in the office after my parents split, was my advocate when I was in middle school. When I got to high school, my history teacher, Mr. Pearson, reached out to me when I was failing. There have been too many advocates in my life for me to name: Ms. DeCoteau when I started teaching; Dr. Castro, who not only gave me space for my youth summits but also helped me with my proposal for Mott Hall; and many more people who did so much for me. All of these individuals poured support into me and in their own way said, "I see you. I hear you."

When my scholars go on to high school, I try to make

sure they all have at least one advocate in their new buildings who will see and hear them. It was like when Eve from P.S. 73 thought she couldn't make it at her new high school—all she needed was someone to take note of her there to make it through. When Antonne decided to go to City Polytechnic High School of Engineering, Architecture, and Technology, I had Mr. McLeod take him to the school to meet the principal, Yusef Muhammed, so he could see the investment we were making in his future and, I hoped, form an attachment to him. Just like with Vidal and the rest, all I can do is give them the opportunity to have an advocate.

The scholars become like my children, and like any parent I never stop worrying about their social and emotional development. Mott Hall graduates continue to hang out at school—during holidays, summer break, after hours—because we are a family.

We can't get rid of them. And I'm fine with that. Even though we go through a rigorous process of finding them the best high schools that fit each of them individually, we're constantly following up on them to make sure that they're okay. As I said, these *are* our children—and we want to make sure they're successful.

When they leave here, everything I say over and over finally resonates—you won't find adults who will stop and sit and talk to you; it will be up to you to figure out what you don't know; you will be on your own.

Vincent returned with Al, another Mott Hall scholar who graduated in 2014, during their high school freshman year because they had a half day off before the Regents exams. Sitting in one of the purple cushion chairs in my office, Al told me, "I went to Mr. Principal and said thank you."

When Al came to us, he had already been held back. Originally from Jamaica, he'd moved to Brooklyn with his mother and hated it. The fact that he had trouble in school didn't make the adjustment any easier. It was clear to us he needed special services, but his mother wouldn't agree to the assessment. She thought he was being lazy, which is not an uncommon belief of people from certain traditional cultures, like those in the Caribbean, where there isn't a lot of education about or understanding of learning disabilities. People from these cultures often internalize their children's learning problems as their failure as parents instead of seeing them as a disability—just as Al's mom did.

Like most children who struggle in school, Al felt bad about himself. But instead of understanding that and asking for help, he tried to pretend like he didn't care, like he had better things to do. He developed a relationship with Mr. Principal, but when he stopped applying himself, the teacher took it personally. I told him not to, but teachers are humans too. So the two of them stopped talking.

"When did you do that?" I asked about Al's thanking him.

"Just now, like ten minutes ago," he said. "I have to admit I felt like I wanted to cry."

"What did Mr. Principal say?"

"Thank you."

"Teachers don't get to hear that a lot."

I loved my second graduating class because they took the initiative and knew what they wanted. When they wanted a student government, a group of them came to me with a petition. "We got names and individuals who agree with us," they said.

"What? You didn't have to get a petition."

"It's really the entire grade."

"Okay. You can have it."

Still, they kept going. They were go-getters. I like to think that it was because they understood what it means to be at Mott Hall.

When I asked Al how high school was going, though, he admitted he was struggling.

"Do you ask for help?"

"I do. I asked everyone for help, but no one will help you."

I believed him.

"Why haven't you been here for help?" I asked.

"I watch my baby nephew every day after school."

"Where's your sister at?"

"She's locked up."

"Uh-huh."

I looked at Vincent and asked how he was doing in school.

"I've improved a lot," he said.

"What does that mean?"

"Seventy-fives."

"How can we move that up?"

He shrugged his shoulders.

"It's not a great learning environment," he said. "The assistant principal said, 'We have a school filled with ignorant and retarded kids.' So I said, 'Why would you open a school for ignorant and retarded kids?' She just said, 'That's not my problem; I already have four degrees.'"

I put my head in my hands. The students at Vincent's high school were far from angels, but that didn't excuse the assistant principal. Who talks to kids like that? But I only despaired for a second; then I picked my head back up and saw Vincent, a boy who's had a restraining order out on him after he broke another scholar's jaw, now a young man with expectations for himself. When Vincent had asked his assistant principal why there was a school for "ignorant and retarded kids," he was doing what we trained him to do at Mott Hall—to advocate for himself and voice when he felt like he wasn't being treated fairly or with respect.

Those are the proud moments, when scholars, even the ones who barely squeaked through, return to tell me that the lessons we gave them are finally taking root. Rachelle, from Mott Hall's first graduating class of girls—the ones who set fire to the bathroom—came back to show me her report card: all 80s and 90s. The girl who told me over and over, "I can't make it. I can't do this," had returned to say, "I get it, Ms. Lopez. I get that I have to study. I can do it." Success isn't that they no longer have to struggle. The children who pass through this school will always struggle. Success is when they have the confidence and resilience to know they *can* struggle.

I asked Vincent and Al, "What do you need from me? How can I help with your transition in high school? What do I need to put into place to support you all?"

"Help with work," Vincent said.

"So a Saturday program," I said.

"Yeah," both boys answered.

We worked out that they would come to Mr. Principal's Saturday preps for the Common Core math test to get some extra help for their algebra Regents. It wasn't perfect—I would have liked to be able to give them more—but it was better than nothing. The young men stood up and walked to the door. I had been happy to see them graduate, but a part of me wishes I could have kept them here, protected. "You come back if you struggle," I yelled from my desk when they were no longer in sight.

Our work with children is never done. And we can't do that work without the necessary resources. After Vidal appeared on *Humans of New York* and the press picked up the story, we raised more than a million dollars to go to Harvard, create a summer program, and fund future scholarships. People also started to fund materials my teachers had put up on DonorsChoose.org, an online charity where public school teachers across America post requests for materials they need for their classes. Ms. Ferdinand, who teaches sixth-grade science and runs the science club, received organs, dissecting tools, and a document camera to model dissections. Ms. Powell got a set of the novel *Divergent* for her seventh graders "to explore relevant coming-of-age themes like identity, belonging, and group responsibility."

My teachers felt like they had won the Lotto. "I can't believe I have all these things," one said to me. The dynamic shifts when you feel like people are investing in your good. There is more of an incentive to go to work, because there is more to look forward to. The donations made the teachers feel acknowledged as people who are doing valuable work.

It was startling when *Humans of New York* creator Brandon asked us, "What do you need?" because in a Brownsville public school, we're *never* asked what we need. It's more likely that we're told what we need to do— by people who don't know the first thing about our community.

When Vidal was invited to Washington to meet the president, I took the opportunity to put my long-standing question—"What is the thought process behind these national education policies?"—directly to the person in charge. After our meeting at the Oval Office, I jumped in a cab to see Arne Duncan, the U.S. secretary of education.

"You know, you all come up with these ideas, right here, at the very top," I said. "By the time they get down to me, the state has translated them to what they feel is best for their communities. Then New York City adopts what it wants for its districts. As a principal, I have to try to make sense of it all, in a community with a lot of needs."

Secretary Duncan, sensing my desperation, asked me, "When do you take time for you? We see what you are doing in Brownsville, the hard work you do every day in the trenches. But you have to take care of you in order to be good for everyone else."

While I appreciated the recognition of what it means to be on the front lines of education, I said, "I don't have time to take care of myself when I'm concerned about how much more we have to improve. I don't have the luxury of failing, because if I don't do well, I'm that school-to-prison pipeline. I'm literally leading my scholars into prison if I don't get it right. Those are the stats. I have the highest percentage of kids who are part of the bottom third."

I wasn't asking Washington to do anything I don't do in Brooklyn. Wanting the experts who devised the criteria for Race to the Top—federal grants to incentivize school reform on a state level—or the Common Core standards to spend time in the schools their policies affect so strongly was no different than having my team walk around Brownsville. Once you see the facts on the ground, and maybe even ask people what they need, a whole other picture emerges.

To my mind, those who are going to make the policies actually need to start sitting in classes and having authentic conversations. Not with politicians or community leaders but with the kids, teachers, parents, and principals. But especially they need to talk to the kids. From the mouths of babes—children will always speak truth, because they don't have an agenda the way everyone else does.

If you think a school is chaotic, then ask a student why. Ask the child, "If you struggle, who's here to help you? Who's an adult you can trust?" And if you find that kids speak about only one adult, then start speaking to that one adult. "Why is it that the kids trust you? What's going on in your classroom that's not happening in every classroom?"

As adults we like to put names on things. And nowhere are there more systems, metrics, titles, and labels than in education. But unless you're honest with children, about your emotions, their emotions, the work that's necessary for learning both on your part and on their part, you will not speak to children. Those who really want to help students can't do it without getting to know them.

I'm not against standards, just standardization. Consistency across the board is great in theory, but not every neighborhood is the same. So if you're going to have a global standard, then you need to offer the resources to help everybody operate on the same level. Not only does our country lack the political will to do more to bring up the disadvantaged, but many counties across the nation have proven in the sixty years since *Brown v. Board of Education* that communities don't even want to allocate resources equitably or allow students of color from neighborhoods with lower tax revenues into schools in nearby whiter, richer areas. That's despite study after study after study showing that integration is by far the most successful policy for bringing up the test scores of underserved minority students.

We know what we need to do; we just don't want to do it. We need to attract talented leadership to education with both financial and social incentives, maintain rigorous standards for teachers while providing them with the support to achieve those standards, and allow all children access to equal educational resources.

Until that day, those of us working in places like Brownsville are doing it all by ourselves, using the basic tools of teaching: being present, being repetitive, coming at it from another way, asking many questions, having patience, and not giving up.

We have to do all that with the knowledge that we could lose one of our students at any moment. It's a constant fear of mine that tragically came true on August 30, 2015, when Newshawn Plummer, who attended Mott Hall during the 2013–14 school year, was shot and killed in Far Rockaway, just blocks from where his older brother was shot and killed three years earlier.

Newshawn came to us as an eighth grader, because his mother wanted him to be in a totally different environment than their neighborhood, where her older son was gunned down. When Newshawn arrived, he had no interest in school. Preoccupied with his brother's death, he found it difficult to focus on his work. We provided him with at-risk, grief, and family counseling. He was such a tall young man that when he walked down the hallway he looked like he was nineteen, but when he smiled you could see the little kid in him. When he didn't show up to school, my staff called his mother, who was a really involved parent. She didn't make any excuses for his behavior, and she was responsive to any recommendation we made—from getting him into sports to starting him in a counseling program. Her attitude was however you are helping me I will take it, which was such a refreshing change for us.

Newshawn didn't get to graduate with his class because of his absences, but he attended summer school and was accepted to a ROADS Charter High School, which helps overage and undercredited students get up to speed so they can graduate from high school. He had done a year fine when he went back to Far Rockaway on a summer evening to see old friends . . .

It wasn't more than a few days after he was killed that I was hosting Scholar Day, an event held before school begins for new scholars and their parents to meet the teachers and become familiarized with the building—and with my expectations. I was in the middle of my talk to the parents, pleading with them to be mindful of how precious the lives of their children are by being actively involved in their education, when Coach Randy came to the front of the auditorium and interrupted me.

"Ms. Plummer is here," he said.

I was so surprised that I almost didn't understand what he was saying. But I quickly asked the parents and scholars to excuse me for a second while I found Newshawn's mom.

"I wanted you to hear from me that he died," she said.

I lost Newshawn, and I could lose Antonne. Or Vidal. I could lose any of them at any moment. That's why whatever they need, if I can give it to them I will. If I don't give up on my scholars, they don't give up on themselves. They prove that to me every day.

Malik proved it to me when the Monday after our Harvard trip, and the first day of spring break, I showed up at school at 10:00 A.M. and he was already waiting for me. I asked the security guard how long the boy had been there, and he said since nine. The time I had told him I would be there.

"Did you eat? And don't tell me chips," I asked him.

"I was rushing."

"Chips and soda steal your brain cells."

"But fill your stomach," he said with a laugh.

"I'm not kidding. They steal your brain cells because they are loaded with sugar."

We sat at the big conference room table and started with English. He had only been reading to himself for a few minutes when he picked his head up and said, "I don't understand what I'm reading."

"You don't understand what you're reading?"

"Nope."

"I don't believe that. I believe you know what you're reading but you just don't think."

I made him read the story out loud to me. "Before you get to the multiple-choice reading comprehension questions, tell me what the story's about," I said. Malik gave me a summary. "Okay, so you know what the story's about," I said.

When he got to the multiple-choice questions, however, he answered every single one wrong. We began with the first question, about the emotion of the protagonist. "Go back to the story," I said. "Where'd you find your answer?" He didn't know; he had just guessed. "Read the question again and go back into the story and look for the answer." He got the answer wrong again. I don't know what he was looking at. He didn't know what he was looking at. We were going to have to break the process down further. Patience. Come at it a different way. Don't give up.

"What is the question asking?" I asked.

He mumbled.

"Basically, you're looking for what?"

"How the person feels?"

"Right. Go back and look at the story, find the evidence, then answer the question."

He got it right.

"Why do you think that? I'm not disagreeing, I just want to know your thoughts."

Malik was able to explain how his answer was an emotion and point back to the sentence in the story as proof. I looked at him and said, "Stop. We need to just . . . Can I be honest with you?"

"Yes," he said.

"I have to apologize because you sat in classes where there are all of these adults and no one reinforced that you were smart. So you don't believe in your success and will tell me the wrong answer to every question. But with just a little bit of thinking, you can give me the right answer and tell me why your answer is right.

"Malik, stop second-guessing yourself. Every time you read, you're going to summarize the story first. What is the story really saying? And *then* you go for the questions.

When you look at them, ask yourself, What is the question asking me to do?"

He continued to work on English, mostly on his own. After that we did math and science, broken up by social studies. We left school together at 6:00 P.M.

The next day Malik was waiting for me again when I got to school. We worked on multiplying double-digit numbers, and again he was getting every answer wrong. While watching him, I realized he knew his multiplication tables. There are kids who don't even have this fundamental skill in middle school. But Malik was getting the single-digit multiplication aspect of the more complex problems correct. What I discovered from sitting with him one-on-one though, was that he kept on forgetting the placeholder. In multidigit multiplication problems, you have to constantly move your numbers over as you go along. Malik was putting his digits right underneath one another. It was just a little error, really, but no one corrected him. Somebody didn't check his homework. Somebody didn't stop him and say, "Nope. Go back. Do it again."

That small error meant he would get all his math wrong, whether it was fractions or decimal points. Without the use of placeholders solidly in his set of foundational skills, he would always struggle. His previous math teacher had said that Malik didn't know how to multiply, but he did. He just didn't know the reason why he was supposed to use a placeholder. That's a totally different conversation.

He did not need to do multiplication drills. He needed somebody to force him to remember what to do when he worked with multiple digits, check his work, and show him how to do it again when he got it wrong—which is what we spent the morning doing. Repetition. Patience. Don't give up.

Malik and I went over the concept of placeholders. I did some sample problems, and then he gave it a try. After all that, he continued to forget the placeholder.

"Malik, why are you forgetting the placeholder?"

"I don't know."

"So what's the right answer?"

He went back and got the right answer.

"What was the difference?"

"I don't know."

"What do you mean, you don't know? Yes you do. You just did it! You are sabotaging yourself. So I need you to stop doing that."

On Wednesday, Malik practiced Common Core literature from the official Pearson workbook. The story he was reading—using our method of first doing it out loud, then going to the questions—was "Stolen Day," by Sherwood Anderson. The young black boy from Brownsville plowed through the story by the American writer, whose spare style reflected the vernacular of small-town rural life in the 1940s. "'I stayed there until Mother came up,'" Malik read. "'I knew it would be a long time before I heard the last of the inflammatory rheumatism. I was sick all right, but the aching I now had wasn't in my legs or in my back.' "

I couldn't imagine a piece of writing capturing the imagination of my scholar *less* than this one. I was having trouble staying awake. But when Malik went to answer the first multiple-choice question, he got it right.

"Very, very good!" I said.

A little smile appeared on his face. Malik has a very nice smile. Then he got the next answer right.

"Look at you! Go ahead, go ahead."

When I told him he got the third answer right—three out of three—the look on his face was priceless. He was so happy. Learning for learning's sake, this was the reward.

Just then two lively Mott Hall graduates popped into the room. One of them was Jessica, the girl who'd lost her mom when she was here and preferred to remain in school rather than go home.

"My girls!" I squealed before introducing them to Malik.

"Oh, you have a while to go," said Sabella, a pretty girl with aspirations of becoming a plus-size model.

"Yeah, but he's learning," I said.

"It's going to be a journey," she said.

Malik, with a reputation for a bad attitude, was waiting for me at school each morning of that spring break, and he stayed until I left, at 6:00 P.M. He wasn't doing it with any ulterior motive; the Harvard trip was already over. No, this kid wanted to understand his schoolwork and learn. And he did. He may have struggled with getting a single answer right one day, but the next he was getting them *all* right.

What it took was sitting with him and proving he could do it by employing all those fundamentals of teaching: *being present, being repetitive, coming at it from another way, asking many questions, having patience,* and *not giving up.*

He just needed me to say "Open up the book" and "Do it again." Half the time I didn't give him as much one-on-one attention as he could have used, because of people who came and went all day long. People show up even during holidays to get help with something, complain, or just for a hug from me. Still, Malik accomplished so much simply by sitting by my side, practicing the strategies I showed him, producing work, and having me check his answers. The greatest lesson I taught Malik that week wasn't placeholders or how to answer reading comprehension questions but not to take the easy way out by saying, "I can't do this." Facing academic challenges is the only way to build resiliency in school, just as it is on the street.

When I ask the scholars and their parents, "What's different about our school and the school you went to before you arrived here?" 99 percent of the time the answer is "Someone cares about me here."

I can't give a formula for how to achieve that, other than to say my work will always be about putting the children first. Whether it's one-on-ones with children, professional development with teachers, meetings with parents, or whole-community conversations, I'm just relentless about that vision.

That's why the first thing that popped into my mind while I was working with Malik was *How long have you been sitting in your classroom, making the same mistake?* His teachers might be doing right by all the other kids in the room, but if there is one scholar in their space who isn't getting it—I have a problem with that. I heard all the complaints about Malik, primarily that he had such a negative attitude. He had a negative attitude because someone failed him. When he told me in my office that afternoon before the Harvard trip that "I always fail," he was just modeling what the adults in his life had showed him.

Malik was in a contained classroom for scholars with individualized education plans, with two teachers, so I really didn't understand how he wasn't getting what he needed. I decided to send my weekly e-mail to the staff on Friday, because they were going to need three days to recuperate from it. Oh, it was going to be heavy. And when they returned from spring break, it was going to be a tense week, because I would be asking questions, going into classrooms, and pulling work sheets to understand exactly why Malik wasn't learning.

I eat, drink, sleep, and breathe my work because I want

to know that what I do matters. It's because my expectations are so high that as soon as anyone walks into Mott Hall, he or she can tell this is not a place where anything less-than will be tolerated. I also put so much into my work because I try to provide the children in my care with everything that will allow them to thrive.

It all begins with listening to them. That's the power behind *Humans of New York*. When was the last time somebody asked you a question and seriously listened to your answer? We never get too old for that.

Listening, however, isn't a passive act. When Malik came to me and laid himself bare by saying, "I don't understand. I'm failing," I honored his voice and proved I heard him by validating his frustrations and working with him to overcome them. The week we spent together at Mott Hall will not save him, but it'll remain a valuable lesson long after his middle school years are done.

Malik is part of a village, and we will not let him fail. By the time he's in eighth grade, he'll be a totally different person. That I'm sure of. In the meantime, however, he knows, the next time he feels so angry in class that he wants to act out, he can stand up and say, "I'm going to see Ms. Lopez. I'll be back."

When he comes to my office, he can sit down and he doesn't have to say a word—I'll deal with his teachers for him. Knowing he has a safe space where someone always has his back is all he needs to shift his outlook. He can say, "I believe in myself because my principal cares about me." I do, just as I believe in all my scholars. Because every child can learn, every child matters, and every child should have the chance to walk across the bridge to brilliance.

ACKNOWLEDGMENTS

Educators have the power to influence generations. Unfortunately, many go unrecognized despite their passion and dedication to this hard work. I stand in honor of those outstanding individuals and my ancestors who have paved the way by opening doors that were once closed. I am eternally grateful for my family and all of the beautiful souls who have traveled this life's journey with me. There are simply too many to mention.

To all of my scholars, those past and present, thank you for teaching me the importance of being a voice in the fight for equity and access in education.

To my MHBA staff, I salute you for working against the odds and being present on behalf of our scholars. I thank you for your time and dedication.

To my assistant principal, Karen Cadogan, my prayer warrior, you are an extraordinary work partner.

To the New York City Department of Education, thank you for the opportunity to open a school that cultivates "Brownsville brilliance."

To Karen St. Hilaire, thank you for guiding my magic— and Diane, we "BEAT STAGE THREE."

To my SOULSISS and BKLYN Combine family, thank you for encouraging me to live in my truth and being a source of strength that keeps me grounded.

Brandon, you are undoubtedly the voice of humanity and I am eternally blessed to be a part of the *Humans of New York* legacy.

Rebecca, you have been more than a collaborator; you are an amazing being who never compromised the integrity and authenticity of my voice while writing my story.

To the team at Viking/Penguin, words cannot express my gratitude for allowing me the platform to share my story with the world.

Lastly, to Monique Achu, my trusted friend and confidante, there is no one else on earth capable of building the "bridge to brilliance" with me.